Breaking the Chains of
TRANSGENERATIONAL TRAUMA

*My Journey from
Surviving to Thriving*

DOROTHY HUSEN, LMFT

AUTHORITY
PUBLISHING

Copyright © 2020 by DOROTHY HUSEN
All rights reserved.

No part of this publication may be reproduced, stored in a retrieval system, or transmitted in any form or by any means, electronic, mechanical, scanning, recording, photocopying, or otherwise, without the prior written permission of the author.

Limit of Liability/Disclaimer of Warranty: This publication is designed to provide accurate and authoritative information in regard to the subject matter covered. It is sold with the understanding that neither the author nor the publisher is engaged in rendering legal, investment, accounting or other professional services. While the publisher and author have used their best efforts in preparing this book, they make no representations or warranties with respect to the accuracy or completeness of the contents of this book and specifically disclaim any implied warranties of merchantability or fitness for a particular purpose. No warranty may be created or extended by sales representatives or written sales materials. The advice and strategies contained herein may not be suitable for your situation. You should consult with a professional when appropriate. Neither the publisher nor the author shall be liable for any loss of profit or any other commercial damages, including but not limited to special, incidental, consequential, personal, or other damages.

BREAKING THE CHAINS OF TRANSGENERATIONAL TRAUMA
My Journey from Striving to Thriving
By DOROTHY HUSEN, LMFT
1. PSY022040 2. SEL001000 3. HEA009000
ISBN: 978-1-949642-47-6
EBOOK: 978-1-949642-48-3

Cover design by Clare Finney

Printed in the United States of America
Authority Publishing
11230 Gold Express Dr. #310-413
Gold River, CA 95670
800-877-1097
www.AuthorityPublishing.com

Dedication

For all our inner children who have survived for us.

TABLE OF CONTENTS

Introduction: The Bitch — 6

Chapter 1: Trauma? What Trauma? — 9

Chapter 2: What I Needed But Didn't Get. — 20

Chapter 3: Trauma Begets Trauma — 27

Chapter 4: Why Does This Keep Happening to Me? — 38

Chapter 5: Lost Connection — 46

Chapter 6: False Prophets — 56

Chapter 7: A Match Made in Trauma — 74

Chapter 8: Trauma: The Next Generation — 88

Chapter 9: Re-parenting Myself — 102

Chapter 10: The Spiral — 115

Chapter 11: An Identity of My Own — 125

Chapter 12: Intergenerational Healing — 132

Chapter 13: Thriving — 142

Acknowledgements — 148

Introduction

THE BITCH

"Trauma is a bitch," said the young man. "Yes, yes, it is," I replied, as I stepped down from the podium. I'd just delivered a talk on trauma and mind/body psychotherapy to an audience of atheists at their monthly "Skipping Church" event.

Ten years earlier, I couldn't have imagined speaking in front of such a group. (Or any group, if I'm being honest.) And certainly not on the topic of psychotherapy. Ten years earlier, I'd seen myself as a homemaker. The wife of a successful attorney in Southern California. The mother of two teenagers. And most significantly, a Christian woman, sure Jesus could and would heal whatever ailed me—with no need of or tolerance for any kind of psychiatry.

But the truth was and is more complex than that. Because trauma is complex. It can grow from one single event in a moment or a series of smaller events over a lifetime…or, in my case, both. Worse, unknown to (or more accurately, suppressed by) me, my trauma had not only held me back from fully living for five decades, it had perniciously infected my children, stunting their lives as well.

And that's the real "bitch" of trauma. The contagiousness of the emotional states it creates. Transferred through our relationships. It becomes transgenerational, passing from parent to child.

My desire to write this book began when my own healing journey from transgenerational trauma took a deep dive (a nice way of saying I had an emotional breakdown). Just before my "deep dive," I was a practicing trauma therapist, soon to become a licensed marriage and family therapist. As part of my education, I was in therapy myself and doing well. I'd become fully aware of my childhood trauma and the affect it had had on my life. Step by step, I was coming into my own, experiencing a more honest relationship with my husband, and modeling healthier behaviors for my children. Then, my elderly mother moved into our home. And down I went. Reverting to old patterns, regressive behaviors, reactive thinking. The individuated me I'd worked so hard to realize was slipping away. After eighteen months of living with Mom, I found myself at a rehabilitation center 3,000 miles away from home.

Having to enter a rehab facility made me feel like a failure. But I'd soon come to understand that was just my ego talking, trying to limit me once again. In the four weeks I was there, I read (practically devoured) three books written for daughters with controlling mothers. At first, these books helped me feel normal. They let me know I wasn't alone. That what I'd experienced and felt wasn't crazy. That *I* wasn't crazy. They gave me hope.

But as I really digested them and talked through them in therapy sessions, I saw there was more going on in this dance between my mother and myself than I'd understood before. And it went way deeper than a controlling mother and a dutiful daughter. I came to see the connection between my trauma and the security I looked for from all the relationships in my life—but primarily and most especially from my relationship with my mother.

With that breakthrough, the pieces of my trauma story began to fall into place more clearly than ever. For the first time, I saw my path forward. A path that would lead to my getting that sense of security I craved from one relationship—the most important relationship of all— my relationship with myself.

This book is the story of my walking that path. I start by explaining how the different types of trauma often take root from events and relationships in our childhoods. How, if we don't fully deal with our traumas, they express themselves throughout our lives—and how such expressions dictated my life. Using science and psychology, we can demystify our trauma, allow ourselves to explore it for what it is and without shame. Then, I show you how I healed from my trauma. And how you can too. Breaking the cycle of trauma for ourselves and our families.

Healing our trauma isn't an easy thing to do. Mostly because the fear trauma produces feels warranted, comfortable, and even normal to us. And what is required to neutralize that fear feels off, uncomfortable, and maybe even wrong. Because what's required is love. Not the whimsical, euphoria of romantic love. Not the hero's sacrificial love. Not the deep, instinctual love of a parent for a child. But self-love.

As you walk with me through my story, learn the science and research of trauma, and see that self-love can be developed, my hope is that you too find your path to healing. That you realize you're not alone. That you begin to see yourself with kindness and compassion. That you see your path forward, eventually falling in love with yourself so hard that you break the bitch that is transgenerational trauma. And you emerge from this life journey, as I did, with only love and healing to pay forward to your children and grandchildren.

Chapter 1

TRAUMA? WHAT TRAUMA?

"Dorothy, I think you have PTSD."
Silence.
"Post Traumatic Stress Disorder."
Silence.
Anne, my first therapist, had a kind face and was comfortable with long silences. She sat across from me in her office with her little dog at her feet and let those words sink in. I looked out the window at the beautiful, large trees on this sunny Southern California day, and I knew she was right. I had PTSD. I felt confused and relieved at the same time. There had been moments in the past forty-eight years of my life that I suspected something was wrong with me.

"But how could what happened when I was a kid still affect me now?" I asked.

"Well, let's look at how your symptoms align with the diagnosis of Post Traumatic Stress Disorder in the DSM-5."

My body relaxed. This was the real reason I was in therapy. To learn more about how therapists do their work—not to be psychoanalyzed myself.

"Okay, "I said. She picked up the big gray book and sat down next to me.

I had my own DSM-5—*Diagnostic and Statistical Manual of Mental Health Disorders, 5th Edition*—on my home-office bookshelf, along with the other psychology textbooks my husband, Jim, and I had purchased for our classes. We'd both recently gone back to school to become licensed marriage and family therapists. One of our first course requirements was six months of personal psychotherapy.

I'd explained all that to Anne when we set up the appointment. "I only need therapy to satisfy my course requirement," I'd said. "My life is good. I don't need therapy. It's only for school."

After all, Jim and I were successful by anyone's standards. We'd been happily married for twenty-some years. Our children were grown. His law practice supported us well. Now we were transitioning together to careers in psychotherapy—which would be less demanding on Jim. And anyway, if I ever did have a problem, I would turn to my Bible and Jesus for help, not to the DSM-5 and certainly not to a therapist.

With the manual open to PTSD, she handed me the form I'd filled out in her waiting room.

"Look at your answer to this question," she said. She pointed to: "Did you experience any sexual abuse as a child?"

My body immediately stiffened as the familiar rush of darkness closed in around my vision. I knew what I'd written, and I didn't want to look at my answer. I could feel my heart beating in my mind as I stared stiffly forward.

"Your handwriting is small and uneven. It looks like a child wrote that answer," she continued.

I looked. She was right. I saw three crooked lines of sentences that crawled up into the margin. It was difficult to read. It didn't even look like my handwriting.

As we sat silently side by side, my mind drifted back ten years, the last time I tried to talk to someone about what had happened to me. I couldn't remember her name, but I pictured her clearly, a young thirty-something mom who taught women's Bible study at my church.

I admired her—a mother of two girls, the wife of one of our respected elders. She stood on stage in front of us and shared how she had been sexually molested when she was a child. She finished her sermon with a beautiful ending: Jesus touched her, healed her pain, and mended her broken heart. Afterward, all the women in the room were quiet. Not many women in church shared about sexual abuse. We all felt a little uncomfortable.

The next morning, I wrote her an email. Then I deleted it. Then I wrote another one—laboring over every word. I went back and forth like that for hours. Finally, I told myself it was now or never, and I just laid my trauma story out there. Some desperate force inside me wanted help. I pushed the send button—and left for work.

At work, I couldn't stop thinking about my email. I thought about her receiving it. I envisioned her reading every word and thought about how she might respond to me. After work, I came home and checked my inbox. Nothing. Hmm, she probably hadn't read it yet. Every day, I checked and re-checked and then checked again. Nothing. No response.

I felt horrible and embarrassed. Then I worried what she thought of me.

The next week at Bible study, I couldn't look her in the eye. I glanced shyly one time. She looked at me. I quickly lowered my eyes. Part of me hoped she would come over and talk to me. That she would notice me. Maybe, she'll ask me to pray with her or invite me to lunch or something. Yet, I kept my head down and my eyes averted.

Nothing happened that day or any day in the following weeks. Eventually I stopped waiting for her to respond. I buried the whole bad memory away—something I was pretty skilled at.

When I think back on that email now, I realize why she never responded. What I wrote—which I thought was so personal and revealing—was an attempt to please (or maybe even impress) someone I admired. With every carefully worded revision, I minimized my trauma further. I even tied it all up with a happy ending. I wrote that Jesus had healed me too—which wasn't true. She hadn't reached out to help me because I hadn't asked for help. I'd presented her with a story that fit comfortably into her worldview and mine.

Now here I was with Anne sitting next to me. A person who wanted to help me, to talk to me about what really happened. And I couldn't open my mouth.

Anne turned to "Symptoms of Post Traumatic Stress Disorder" and read a few out loud:

You experienced a life-threatening event.

You experience flashbacks as if the event is happening again.

You avoid memories of the event.

You minimize the event.

I retreated to my silence. "It's okay," Anne said. "You don't need to talk about anything you don't want to talk about. We can talk about psychology and what you're learning in school." As she closed the book, she said, "But, Dorothy, do you think you could start writing about what happened to you? Have you ever journaled before?"

My head popped up, I met her eyes, and suddenly found my voice. "Yes, I journal every day for my quiet time with God," I announced.

Anne smiled. "Great. During that time, why don't you start writing down what you remember."

I pulled back instinctively and thought, "What? Give up my routine with God? What would He think? I'm not sure." For twenty-five years I'd followed the same morning routine. I read my Bible and then wrote about what I'd read.

I looked at Anne. She was still smiling, waiting for me. I sighed deeply, "Okay, I'll try it."

The next morning, I opened my Bible, then closed it. I opened my journal and began writing.

WHAT I REMEMBERED

The following is my first journal entry verbatim:

This is my first memory. The first day of my life.

I am little. Six years old. I was walking home from school. I am walking on the sidewalk when I am surprised to see an older boy to the right coming toward me and he is calling out to me and waving for me to come to him. I stop and say, "What?" I was confused. I didn't know this boy and I couldn't understand what he was saying.

He came closer to me and I could understand what he was saying, "Your brother told me to come get you and bring you to him."

I say again, "What?"

The boy said again, "He's right behind those trees. He's waiting for you. And wants me to take you to him. He's going to be mad at you if you don't come."

I thought to myself with a smile, "My brother must be up to something funny." I decide to follow him.

The boy leads me into the trees and helps me down a hill. We are under a bridge. I notice the air gets cooler here. I keep wondering what my brother wants. Where am I? And where is my brother?

The boy turns around to face me, bends down and begins to unbutton my dress. I pull back and try to push his hands away. He grabs my shoulders. He is strong. He shakes me and hurts me and says "No!"

He is no longer smiling. I'm scared. I'm confused. Where is my brother? What is going on? Why is he taking my clothes off where anyone can see me? I feel very scared and embarrassed. I've never been outside naked in front of a stranger before. What if someone sees me? I keep looking for my brother and asking, "Where is my brother?"

I'm laying down on the ground. The ground is uncomfortable, rocky, and cold. I'm looking up and see underneath a concrete bridge. I'm not sure. I can feel him spreading my legs apart. I don't understand...why? What is he doing? I feel pressure as he touches me where I go to the bathroom. He spits on me. Why? I must be dirty. Mommy spits on a napkin to clean dirt off my face. I keep looking up and try to lay still. Then nothing, just blackness, no memories. I hear some kids laughing far away. The man jumps up. He puts his hand over my face and I see his eyes right in front of me and he says, "Don't say anything."

I'm scared. I can't breathe. He's holding my neck and I can't breathe. I think, "I'm dying. I cry out for my mom. "Mommy!" I know I am going to die. Then blackness again.

Next memory is that I'm not dead. I'm confused. The man is holding me up. He is helping me to put my clothes back on. He is scared again. And I am confused again. He says over and over, "Don't tell anyone. Promise me you won't tell anyone. Don't tell anyone. Ok? Promise? Promise me."

I nod yes, okay. He makes me say, "I promise." I say it. Then he takes me by the hand and leads me back to the sidewalk. He tells me to go home and not say anything.

As I'm walking away, I turn around to look where he is. He is still standing there watching me. Then he waves and smiles and calls out, "Promise?" I nod yes and say, "Yes, I promise."

Then in my head I think to myself, "I'm going to tell my mom."

Next memory is sitting on the couch next to my mom. I feel like I'm in trouble. I feel scared because my mom is angry. My mom is not happy with me. She doesn't say anything, at least, I don't remember if she said anything. I remember sitting next to my mom waiting for something, but I don't know what. We are sitting and waiting, but for what?

For the next six months, I wrote down everything I could remember. Some days I couldn't stop writing and even stayed home from work.

Once a week, I brought my journal in for Anne to read. I sat silently and watched her read it. We didn't talk about it. Instead, we filled the remaining time discussing what I was learning in school, as she'd promised.

Instinctively or by training or by some miracle, Anne knew I could write what I could not yet speak. She also knew it was important for me to watch her read the secrets I'd hidden away my whole life. And after just a few weeks of this unspoken exchange, a strange thing happened...I began to feel better, a bit more at ease in the world.

That was the start of my healing journey from trauma.

HOW WE MAKE SENSE OF WHAT HAPPENS

When we are children, we learn about ourselves and the world mostly from our parents. From birth, we look to them for survival, to keep us safe, to help us navigate life. So whatever they tell us about how things work, how we work, we take it as gospel truth and integrate it into our worldview. Typically, we don't question what we're told until life challenges us to.

For instance, the first time I got car sick, I thought that I felt hunger. My dad was driving us up a twisty mountain road. I cried and told my parents I was hungry. They told me I'd be able to eat when we got to the top, which wouldn't be long. When we got out of our car, my "hunger" went away. I felt better. My parents were irritated.

But when we drove down the mountain, I started crying and saying I was hungry again. My mom looked me straight in the eye and told me that I wasn't hungry, I was car sick. Which was a revelation to me, a new piece of knowledge I now owned. Good information that I still use to this day.

We learn about our emotions the same way. Our parents or caregivers talk to us about what we're feeling. Through this back and forth conversation, we begin to know our emotions, understand them, and, if all goes well, learn to manage them ourselves.

Problems occur when our parents don't talk to us about our feelings—leaving us confused or worse, with a dangerous misinterpretation of what's going on inside us. Equally as damaging is when our parents usurp our emotions and talk to us only about their feelings, not ours. Instead of coming to know our own emotions, we adopt their feelings for our own—which causes us to have misbeliefs about ourselves.

My mom always told me that I was peaceful and praised me for it.

She'd tell me my peaceful personality was her gift from God. It made me feel good when she talked like this. I was proud to be peaceful. So I adopted her feeling and allowed it to define me. Decades later in therapy, I came to see that I wasn't peaceful at all. I was anxious—scared of my mother's anger. My peacefulness was a coping mechanism for anxiety, not a gift from God.

MAKING SENSE OF A TRAUMA

Understanding all this now, it makes perfect sense that when invited in that first therapy session to talk about my childhood sexual abuse, I literally didn't have the words. That's because that huge, confusing event had been fully processed by six-year-old me alone and then preserved in my mind that way.

In addition to my six-year-old's limited life experience, I was shy and quiet—I didn't go looking for adventure. I was in first grade, just learning to read and write basic words and sentences, so of course my vocabulary was limited.

So when my six-year-old body and brain were thrust into a terrifying event, all I could compute was that my body was injured and my brain was frightened. I didn't have the experience to understand much beyond that. And I certainly didn't have the language to make sense of it.

As it turns out, no one else around me in 1967 had the language to help me make sense of it either. Unfortunately, the adults in my life—my parents, the police officer who investigated, the doctor who examined me afterward—seemed more focused on the event than taking care of me. (This was no one's fault. It's just how it was at that time. Today, authorities are much more attuned to victims' emotional needs.) I could see and feel they were all very agitated. But no one explained to me why. Even my mom didn't talk to me about it—not the day I told her, not after the police left, and not after the doctor visit. Not ever. She ignored it, so I ignored it.

Left to think this through for myself, what six-year-old Dorothy concluded was, "Gosh, I've really upset the adults in my life with this news. I did something wrong. I'm bad. I'm dirty. I better not tell anyone about this ever again." And with that I buried the memory as deep as I could because I could not bear the pain and the shame of it.

As I grew older, of course, my critical thinking and verbal skills increased. But I didn't bring that memory up for a rewrite. Like most trauma survivors, I arranged my life to keep those bad thoughts hidden, along with the bad feelings they generated.

When I showed up in Anne's office, I was not expecting that question on her intake form—"Did you experience any sexual abuse as a child?" I was triggered. Without warning and beyond my control, my body was filled with the disgust and shame I'd connected to that memory of terror and pain. All of which was made visible by the tiny, scrawling handwriting of my answer.

Then in the session, when Anne asked me to speak of the abuse, all that emotion stuck in my throat. I froze, like a deer in the headlights. Which she picked up on immediately, and so she allowed me to process the event by writing about it.

REWRITING MY PAST

Privately writing down my memories gave me the space to bring those memories up from the deep without worry of outside judgment and to put a new, grown-up narrative on them. It allowed me to integrate my six-year-old's feelings of terror, shame, and confusion with my adult wisdom of what I now knew about sex and sexual abuse.

Then, by reading my journal silently in front of me, Anne validated my words, my emotions, and my new understanding of those events. I could feel her thinking: "Yes, that's right, Dorothy. That happened to you. Yes, you felt scared. You felt embarrassed. You felt humiliated. You felt confused."

It's no wonder that each week, I felt better and better. Journaling opened some kind of pressure valve in my mind. I slowly began to let go of the feelings of shame and disgust I'd created as a child. I felt better in a way that I'd never experienced.

Like so many of my peers, I'd learned from my World War II era parents not to look back, not to go digging up past troubles. This was reinforced by the fervent brand of Christianity my family practiced: look to Jesus to absolve you of your sins. Not yourself. Repent when you feel ashamed, because surely sin is causing you to feel that way.

Through therapy, I learned a different perspective: shame is an emotion, not a sin. I started to have curiosity and new thoughts. I discovered I felt better when I dug up my past. And I started to wonder why the thousands of times I'd repented my sins had not brought me the peace I was finding in therapy. I questioned the difference between my sin and my shame. And I wrote it all down in my journal.

Most of all, I came to understand that unresolved trauma doesn't leave us, no matter how securely we think we have it buried in our memory. Or how much friends or family members—who may well carry their own traumas—encourage us (overtly or otherwise) to ignore it. Or how fervently we pray to an external spiritual being to heal us. Until it's resolved, trauma remains a destructive undercurrent in our lives. Infecting us and everyone we're in a relationship with. It continues to wreak havoc until we bring it into the light and deal with it.

All we have to be is willing. Finally, I found myself willing.

EXERCISE

Journaling—Same Trauma, Different Story

Journaling is how I started my healing journey. So if you're working toward healing from trauma, I encourage you to try it. Think of journaling as a conversation with your younger self, nothing more. When you journal about a specific event or a memory that feels "off" to you, try creating a back-and-forth conversation between parent and child. By playing both roles, you have the opportunity to replace the voice that's there now with your own wiser adult voice.

Here's how:

- *Step one:* Choose something to journal about, something about yourself—a feeling, a reaction, a behavior, some past event—you want to explore.
- *Step two:* Sit down with a notebook and start writing for as long or short a time as you wish.
- *Step three:* You can write on one topic for as many sessions as you wish or change topics. (There really aren't any rules.)
- *Step four:* Try to make journaling a daily practice. Or at the very least, something you do whenever you feel tense, confused, or upset.

No one needs to read what you've written; even you don't have to read it. You don't have to go back and analyze anything you don't want to. Just getting it out of your mind and onto the paper is enough. Your brain will do the rest (the processing) for you naturally.

Chapter 2

WHAT I NEEDED BUT DIDN'T GET.

The sexual assault occurred in Hawaii. That's where I was born and lived until I turned seven and my family moved to California. I had two older siblings—a brother, Glenn, and a sister, Sadie—and one younger brother, Owen.

Glenn and Sadie were nearly a decade older than I. Owen was four years younger. So my mom became my number-one playmate and confidante. I was devoted to her—and she to me. She would tell stories endlessly of her life growing up in Czechoslovakia and of her family's struggles after World War II. I loved nothing more than to listen to those stories and be in her presence. For hours and hours, we sat in the kitchen together, talking.

"Then what happened?" I'd ask every time my mom paused.

She'd smile at me. "You really want me to tell you more?"

"Yes! Don't stop. Please. Then what happened?"

"Well, alright. Let me refill my coffee and get a cigarette, and I'll tell you more."

Ever since I can remember, that was our dance. She was the leader and I was the follower as we spun around and around together. The last thing I would have ever done was bring up a topic that might upset her and stop the dance.

Following are a few more excerpts from the journal I kept for Anne.

Excerpt 1: The Lady Wearing Men's Clothes
I remember talking to a lady dressed in men's clothes. She's asking me questions about what happened. She's writing stuff down. Who are these people? Why is everyone looking at me and asking me questions? I feel like I've been bad. No smiles. Only angry faces. Everyone whispers. I know they're talking about me. About how bad I've been. I'm in trouble, but I don't know why exactly. I know that I shouldn't have been naked. Where's my mom? I'm scared. What did I do? What's going to happen? I'm scared. What's going to happen?

Excerpt 2: The doctor
The doctor was big and old. He smiled at me, but I don't remember what he said. I do remember he was the only one who smiled at me.

He patted my hand. I am lying on a cold hard table like a bed raised up high above the ground, so that when I turn my head, my mom's face is right there, a little lower than mine. She looks worried. I feel sick to my stomach, and I wish I wasn't here. I wish I could be away from here.

There are other people standing around me. Strangers. Everyone looks angry or mad. I feel so bad. I close my eyes. I want to see blackness. I don't know who they are. No one says anything.

The doctor spreads my legs, just like the older boy did and started touching me again, in the same place, just like before. He is saying something as he is touching me and looking between my legs. He is very serious with a low voice. I can't understand what he is saying or what is happening.

No one else says anything. They are standing around me looking down at me. He is the doctor. I hope he doesn't take too long. I want to go home.

Everyone knows something is wrong with me. I look over at my mom, and she looks very sad. She gives me a smile. We are both embarrassed, ashamed. My mom is not happy. She doesn't want to be here either. All these people are staring at me and no one is saying anything. I don't know what is going on.

Suddenly the doctor is finished. He leaves the room. Everyone is glad to leave, and I am glad they left. I remember feeling relieved to be alone with my mom again and not wanting to remember or think about what just happened. I don't ever want to have to see those people again. I want to cry.

I had never experienced so many strangers looking at my naked body. I didn't even know that I had a vagina. All I knew was this part of my body was how I went to the bathroom and I knew that going to the bathroom was private, not something I did with anyone else watching me except my mom. The shame I felt was shared with the adults who had to watch the procedure. I remembered it as everyone was ashamed of me.

Excerpt 3: Too big for little desks

I'm with the lady dressed as a man again. She is the police, I think, because she is not a teacher. I know that teachers wear dresses. We are in a strange place. She is telling me to point to the older boy, the one who hurt me. I don't know anything else except that I am to point to the older boy. She holds my hand and leads me to a door. She opens the door and we step into a room.

I am shocked. That's him. I'm scared. What's he doing here? Uh-oh, everyone knows. I don't know what to do. I can't move. I just stare at him. And I'm shocked to see him right there. Then I notice two other teenage boys sitting in the room. They look very funny, all three of them are sitting in small chairs connected to desks for little kids. "They're all too big for these chairs," I thought to myself. I remember their long legs scrunched, and they don't fit.

No one saying anything and everyone is looking down. Everyone looks very unhappy. They look like they are in trouble and they are too big to sit in those little chairs.

I remember that I broke my promise to him. I remember promising that I would not tell on him. He knows that I promised, and I've broken my promise. I feel bad. The boy looks at me, and I am scared, but then he looks down. I know he feels bad too. We both feel ashamed. I think we both want to cry. The lady policewoman is nudging me, and I know she wants me to point to him. I walk up to him and I point my finger at him and I look at the policewoman. She asks me, "Is this the boy?" I nod my head, yes. The lady walks towards me, holds my hand, and we walk to the door. I turn and look back at such an odd sight and think to myself how funny they look squished into those little desks with their long legs.

That is the last time I saw the teenager who hurt me, or the policewoman. That was the last time anyone ever talked to me about what happened. Period. From that moment on, everything that happened I could forget. I never, ever wanted to remember what happened again, ever. It was mine and my mom's secret…I was the secret. I became (in my mind) my family's dirty little secret. I must not talk about it. I must not remember it.

Excerpt 4: The chain-link fence…

My family moved to California less than a year later. Now in second grade, I remember being placed in front of the whole classroom. The teacher stood next to me and said that I was a new student from Hawaii. I remember feeling very embarrassed. I hated everyone staring at me and not saying anything. During a break some girls asked me questions about Hawaii—something about grass skirts and naked people. I didn't know the answers to their questions.

During recess or lunch break, I hurried to the chain-link fence that separated my school's playground from the adjacent high-school property. My sister, a high schooler, told me that she would come to see me by the fence. I clung to the fence and stuck my face up to the holes, looked and squinted very hard to try to see my sister.

> The buildings were far away and the teenage kids looked very small. Then I thought I saw her walking towards me. "Yes! It's Sadie. She is coming," I thought. She smiled and waved, and I felt safe.
>
> She sat in the grass right on the opposite side of the fence. She asked me some questions about my school, and I relaxed listening to her voice. When she had to get back, we touched fingers through the chain links.
>
> As I watched her walk away, she turned around and waved at me again. But as she turned her back again, I felt nervous and worried. I didn't want to be left alone with strange kids and a strange teacher.

Notice how disorganized and sometimes incoherent those entries are. How awkward their phrasing. How they jump in tone and tense. When I read them now, I wonder where the facts are, the things anyone would want to know. Who called the police? The doctor? What happened to my assailant? These are details my parents never filled in for me. And I never felt comfortable asking about them, even as an adult.

LEFT ALONE, TRAUMA GROWS

What I've come to understand in my studies and through therapy is that it's not what happened to me, but what didn't happen after I was sexually assaulted that caused my PTSD. As explained in the book *Raising a Secure Child: How Circle of Security Parenting Can Help You Nurture Your Child's Attachment*, human beings all have the basic emotional needs of comfort, safety, connection, belonging, and exploration. When children feel secure these basic needs will be met, their brain is free to devote energy to curiosity and exploring the world. They become children who try new ideas and are not afraid to make mistakes. When they do make a mistake, they don't see it as a personal failing; they learn from it, so they can do better next time. They come to know their strengths and their weaknesses, and are comfortable with who they are. They ask for help. They think outside the box. They're flexible. They're open to working with others to solve problems and find solutions. Most importantly, they have emotional stability, meaning they're not scared to feel their feelings—the positive as well as the negative. From all this, they develop both self-esteem and self-confidence.

As in all things when we're talking about human development, it's not all or nothing when it comes to a child's sense of security. It's a spectrum—which in turn produces a spectrum for emotional stability, self-esteem, and self-confidence.

Parents play a huge role in where a child lands on that spectrum. It starts, of course, with providing those basic emotional needs. It then continues with helping the child put life experiences—good and bad—into perspective as they grow. Parents who are most successful at this are able to place their own emotions about an event aside, attune with what the child is feeling, and reassure the child through the lens of that child's emotions. This is especially crucial when a child has experienced a traumatic event.

When we as parents are relaxed and in a healthy mental state, attuning to our child's needs and seeing the world through their lens almost comes naturally. But when we ourselves are stressed, upset, or worried, it's harder to get out of our own heads. And this is especially true for a parent who's been traumatized.

When the doctor and nurses examined me for evidence of sexual assault, I needed my mom to attune to my feelings and talk to me about what the doctor was going to do to me and why. When the police took me in the room to point to the boy who assaulted me, I needed my mom to attune to my feelings and talk to me about how I felt when I saw him and why I didn't need to worry about "getting him in trouble." When we moved to California, I needed my mom to attune to how frightened I was of new people and a new environment, and that I needed time to adjust. But most of all, I needed her to tell me that the assault wasn't my fault; that I wasn't in trouble; that she wasn't angry with me; that I was safe and secure; and that she loved me.

Her understanding and guidance would have helped me later in life to draw a clear line between sexual assault and sexuality. It would have lifted blame and shame from me in the moment—and for the next forty years. It would have helped to process and neutralize my trauma.

But my mom couldn't do that.

NEED EXERCISE

What Did You Need?

If asked outright, most of us don't know what we would need to heal a childhood trauma and restore feelings of safety and connection in our lives. Why? Because we've never thought about it. Yet, if we don't know what we need, we're not likely to get it or even recognize it should it come into our lives. So this exercise provides the direction, opportunity, and space to define what that need is for yourself:

- *Step one:* Bring a childhood trauma to mind. Breathe. And sit with it for a moment.
- *Step two:* Notice how you think about that trauma. Note what you feel: Fear? Shame? Sadness? Heartbreak?
- *Step three:* What did you—your younger self—need in that moment? Take your time here. Don't rush the answer.
- *Step four:* What did you get? Did you tell an adult? How did they react? Did you keep it to yourself? How did that make you feel?
- *Step five:* Did you get what you needed? If not, what did you need? What would have helped?
- *Step six:* Would it be possible to give what you needed then to yourself now?

Journal all this if you like. Writing often brings clarity.

Chapter 3

TRAUMA BEGETS TRAUMA

When my maternal grandmother, Maria, was a teenager in Germany, she became pregnant by a married man. To keep the baby girl, whom she named Gerhild, she agreed to marry a German widower, Rudolph, who had six children, and to move away from her family to his home in Czechoslovakia. His first wife had died giving birth to a stillborn child.

My grandmother cared for Rudolph and his children, though she said he never warmed to Gerhild. The couple would have three children together—my mother, Olga, was the oldest, born in 1929.

When my mother was ten, Hitler invaded Czechoslovakia. Mom often spoke of the beautiful schools Hitler built, called Gymnasiums. These well-equipped schools were attended only by the children of German nationals, of which my mother was one. She and her classmates were called Hitler Youth, wore soldier uniforms, and were indoctrinated with songs, marching, and a pledge.

While she adored the abundant amenities of her Gymnasium, she felt conflicted because her Czech friends didn't have these advantages at their schools. She didn't understand why. She didn't understand the war. She saw herself more as Czech than German—and she would identify as a Czech for the rest of her life.

By the spring of 1945, my mother's six older half-siblings were grown and on their own. Her younger brother had died in infancy. Only my mother (about to turn sixteen), her younger sister, Elizabeth, and Gerhild remained under their parents' roof. Rudolph had become wheelchair-bound due to a stroke. And Gerhild had a newborn son. The family story is that Gerhild was married to an SS officer (Saal-Schutz, a Nazi guard unit) who was lost at war and never heard from again. To this day, I don't know if that was true or a cover-up for another out-of-wedlock birth in the family.

My mom told me that when the Soviets liberated Prague in May of that year and Germany capitulated in unconditional surrender, Czech mobs took to the streets to hunt down, beat, and kill German nationals. My grandmother decided the family needed to leave the country. She packed their bags and led her family to the train station—only to be stopped along with thousands of other Germans by Soviet soldiers.

My mom and her family were imprisoned in a temporary internment camp, packed shoulder to shoulder, and given only a cup of broth a day to sustain them. Every night, Soviet soldiers came and got German women and girls to rape. I don't know if my mother and Gerhild were among them. My grandfather, along with most of the elderly and very young, died in the camp. Gerhild's little boy, surprisingly, survived.

The family was eventually moved to a farm to labor. There, the Soviet Occupational Headquarters learned that my mother spoke, read, and wrote German and Czech—and had picked up Russian while in the camp. She was reassigned to work as an interpreter.

Though in an office, her days were no easier and were likely more dangerous than on the farm. She was under constant threat by the Russian soldiers. Often drunk, they'd make violent sexual advances toward her. Every hour of every day, she had to remain vigilant and react quickly to avoid assault, rape, or worse. She'd later credit her survival to standing her ground and appearing tough to these men—no matter how scared she was inside. Until the day she died, my mom never trusted anyone who was Russian and held a grudge against those soldiers.

As the months passed, the Soviet Zone was becoming more dangerous for Germans. My grandmother decided my mother should escape to the American Zone. My grandmother packed a knapsack of food for my mom and gave her money for the train ticket to the city closest to the American Zone. She told my mom to find someone on the train to help her, and once she got to the American Zone, to find her Tante Else, my grandmother's sister. My grandmother assured my mom that she and Elizabeth would join her as soon as they could. (Gerhild chose to stay in what would become East Germany, where she remarried and had more children.)

My mom obeyed her mother. She headed to the station and boarded the train. She didn't have permission to travel. But as an interpreter for the Soviets, she did carry work papers with an official stamp. If she were stopped, she'd show those papers, though she feared anyone looking too closely.

On the train, she heard "whispers" from other passengers. "How far to the American Zone?" "Where's the border?" "How long does it take to get there?" "What happens if we get caught?" It seemed like everyone on the train was trying to escape.

Then the train stopped. End of the line. Everyone got off.

As her mother had instructed, my mom searched for someone to help her make the last several miles of the trip and get her across the border. She chose two grey-haired men. Her mother had warned her not to trust young men because they might rape her.

She nervously began walking behind them until she got the courage to ask if she could travel with them. They agreed, and they had a plan for getting to the American Zone.

As the three of them huddled in a café trying to look inconspicuous, the men told her the American Zone lay across an open field at the edge of town, just beyond the tree line. "We'll start walking after dark," one of the men whispered.

In the wee hours of the morning, they found themselves still trudging through the final field. Deep snow drifts had slowed their pace considerably, but the tree line was in sight. At this point in the story, my mom would always say that walking through that snow made her legs feel like heavy logs. Panic and fear were all that kept her going.

As sun began to creep over the horizon, their dark silhouettes stood out against the snow. They were almost to the end of the field when she saw a Russian soldier. And he saw them. They were caught. He pointed his rifle at them and waved for them to come to him. My mom's heart pounded in her chest. "He's going to rape me and kill me," she thought.

My mom said she cowered behind the two old men. She tried to keep her face and hair covered so the soldier wouldn't notice she was a young woman. The soldier commanded they hand over their papers. He then whistled loudly and called out to his nearest comrade, but there was no reply. Then he spoke nervously under his breath, "What am I going to do with them?" He stepped away and whistled again.

The two men only spoke German. But my mom understood everything the soldier was saying. She realized he was scared and unsure about what to do. Emboldened, my mom stepped forward and spoke in Russian, "Sir, my uncles and I are only crossing over to the American Zone to visit my dying mother. We will return once we have said our goodbyes."

She then showed the soldier her work papers and explained, "I must return to Soviet Headquarters to work by Monday. The Commander said I could go to visit my mother. I will return for work."

The soldier looked surprised and simultaneously relieved because my mom spoke Russian. He told my mom to wait there while he checked with his superiors. When he returned, he commanded them, "Go! And run quickly!"

My mom told the German men that they were free to cross the border. She asked them if they had some vodka to give the young Russian for his kindness. They both said, "No, sorry, we don't have any liquor." They ran as fast as they could toward the border—with my mother following.

After walking for a while, the three of them came upon a farmer with a horse pulling a cart of wood.

"Is this the American Zone?" they asked.

"Yes," said the farmer. "Hop in, and I'll take you to town."

The two men hurriedly threw their knapsacks on the wagon. Crack! A bottle broke in their bag and the strong smell of alcohol filled the air. My mom was furious. Those two ungrateful old men had lied. My mom glared at them and scolded, "It serves you right your bottle broke! You are selfish! You got what you deserved!" She would always conclude by saying the two men sheepishly apologized as this brazen teenage girl admonished her elders.

Once on the other side, she found her aunt and established new work papers. Not too long after, she met my dad, a U.S. GI and her one-way ticket out of war-torn Europe. My mom spoke no English, but he spoke German. They married in Germany so that the United States Army would pay for her travel back to the states—and eventually to his home in Hawaii, not yet a state.

She had physically survived post-war Europe. But there was a mental toll to living every day for years with the threat of physical harm and death ever present. A toll that she—and most of her peers—didn't know how to reconcile, and so were burdened with for the rest of their lives and passed along to the next generation.

FOR BETTER AND WORSE: FIGHT, FLIGHT, FREEZE, OR FAINT

When our brains detect a threat, our neocortex shuts down, blocking us from the time-consuming task of critical thought, and enabling us to react quickly and automatically. Cortisol, adrenaline, and other stimulating chemicals shoot through our bodies—commanding us to either fight, fly, freeze, or faint (FFFF). Whatever will eliminate the threat.

This FFFF response evolved to ensure our survival—the one mission the brain puts above all others. It's what helped our ancestors kill the tiger before being killed by it, run from an avalanche, or keep still when a predator was nearby. And it continues to serve us in the modern world. Like when we slam on the brakes before we even register the car in front of us has stopped. Or we instinctively freeze at the sight of a snake. Or without thinking, we pull a pot from a hot burner before it boils over.

This ability to instantly do what needs to be done without conscious thought is made possible by our brain's huge store of procedural memories—memories of both an event and the successful handling of it. Known in psychological terms as "triggers," these memories lie in wait. Then, when our brains sense threat, bam! All systems go. Our neurons automatically head down the path to fight, flight, freeze, or faint. If we use one reaction more than the others, it can become our all-purpose, go-to, default reaction to threat.

When the threat is physical and immediate, the FFFF response is amazing at keeping us safe. But when it's triggered by a perceived emotional threat, it can lead to trouble. That's because with emotional threats, solutions are rarely as simple as fight, flight, freeze, or faint. Typically, they (and thus, we) would be better served if the neocortex could pause our FFFF reaction to emotional threats, allow us to think through all angles, and process the event or issue in context. Unfortunately, it is emotionally traumatized brains that are most unable to recognize the trigger and take that pause.

There's no doubt that my mother's experiences after World War II left her traumatized and that when triggered, her default reaction was to "fight." After all, "fight" had kept her safe from the constant threat of sexual assault for years. But there's also no doubt that after she got to Hawaii, where there were no longer any physical threats to deal with, her automatic fight reaction paradoxically became a threat in itself.

Neither my dad nor life on the island of Oahu was what she expected. At first, they lived with my dad's sister and her husband—who my mom inadvertently insulted almost immediately by cleaning their house. The language barrier only added to the tension with her new family. My father had to translate for her—and getting him to engage and speak at all was proving to be a feat.

At nineteen, my mom found herself living in the middle of the

Pacific Ocean in a society she didn't understand, married to a man she barely knew who barely talked, and part of a family that disliked her. She had food and physical safety, but her fear and vigilance never left her. Emotionally, she remained on edge.

My parents found work as caretakers for a large estate—my mom cooked and cleaned for the family, my dad took care of the grounds. The job came with a cottage. And in no time, my brother and then my sister came along.

As my father found better jobs and they bought a home, my mother continued to struggle emotionally. She took her frustration out on my father mostly—fighting with him over anything she could find to fight about and flying into a rage without warning. Several years into the marriage, her tension reached its pinnacle and she sued him for divorce.

Far from relieving her struggle, the divorce only added to it. A divorced woman in a foreign land with no marketable skills in the mid-twentieth century, she couldn't find a job. Unable to support herself, she lost custody of my siblings—practically unheard of for a mother in the 1950s—piling more shame on the stigma of her divorce.

She then hastily married a man, who quickly became abusive. In time, he would come to punch her so hard she ended up in the hospital with internal bleeding. When I was old enough to hear it, my mom told me this was the lowest point in her life. She had wanted to die.

But just as she had with those Russian soldiers, she found her fight. She divorced the abuser. Then, she swallowed her resistance to my father and remarried him to be with her children—reminiscent of her own mother's marriage to Rudolph.

Her brain's propensity to go into fight mode at the smallest provocation made anger and fear ever-present energies in our home. It had pushed her into the rash decision to divorce my father without a plan or a nickel to her name, and had caused her to marry an abuser. It's also what made her unable to help me.

PASSING THE TRAUMA TORCH

My mother loved me just as much as any "attuned" parent loves their child. But when I told my mom about my assault, it triggered her traumatized brain. She went right for the fight. Most likely, it was she who called the police and the doctor. And I'm sure she was angry. She had no ability to hit pause, consider how I felt, and that I might need something different from her. I might have needed her not to fight, but to console me.

On the other side of that exchange, six-year-old me was conditioned to know when my mom was in fight mode. My brain was triggered and immediately retreated to my default FFFF response. I froze. Just as I did every time she got angry. Just as I had done when I was assaulted. Just as I would do for the next four decades whenever anything or anyone scared me—and believe me, everything and everyone scared me.

Over those next four decades, even the thought of my assault sent my mom's brain into fight mode and mine into freeze. Left without examination or explanation, my shame, embarrassment, and misbeliefs about what had happened festered into PTSD. These automatic, unconscious forces helped shape me into the shy, quiet, dependent person with very little sense of self that I became.

This is how her trauma passed to me and all my siblings in one way or another. When she was triggered, we were triggered. FFFF was our family dynamic, and we all had our role to play. When trauma like my mom's and like mine is left unprocessed, it shows up in our behaviors and affects everyone in our lives, especially our children, until somebody stops it.

None of this explanation is to blame my mother—or me, for that matter. My mother thought she was protecting me. We parents do the best we can with what we know. When we gain new information, we use it.

TRUTH VANQUISHES TRAUMA

When I was young, I thought my mother's stories about the war were exciting, drama-filled adventures. My mom once told the story of her escape to the American Zone to my high-school history class. My classmates came up to thank her. My teacher told me, "Your mom was the best guest speaker I've ever had in my classroom." I beamed with pride. I saw her accomplishment as a reflection on me.

My mom was amazing. And through her, I felt amazing too. I got lost in her stories—quite literally. With every retelling, I felt less need to have my own story.

Today, as an adult, a parent, and a therapist, I find her stories frightening, and I grieve for her and her family. I can't imagine myself as a teenager, or my own daughter, Emma, under constant threat of rape, starvation, and being killed.

I also see the critical role those stories played in creating our relationship pattern and transgenerational trauma. My mom was stuck in her war experiences—as were many survivors—so much so that she was unable to attune to my emotional needs. My emotional experiences were irrelevant to her. And so they became irrelevant to me.

I too was stuck in my mom's stories—where she always had the right answer. My emotional needs were met by supporting and uplifting her, and making her happy. My motivation came only from meeting her needs.

In her stories, Mom was never afraid, weak, or a victim. She was always the fighter, the hero of every tale. Allowing herself to be anything else—to become vulnerable, to honestly accept what had happened to her, to get behind her anger, to admit she might be wrong sometimes—was not a place her traumatized brain was willing to go, much less to explore and process.

I knew that my sexual abuse caused her pain. I knew she didn't want to talk about it. So to keep her from being hurt and to keep her liking me, I kept silent. My sexual abuse became our unspoken secret. I knew that she knew, and she knew that I knew. But that's as far as it went.

When I got older, I assumed my dad and older siblings knew about my assault. But I wasn't sure, again, because no one ever talked about it. To this day, I have not asked either sibling if they know.

My mom was a woman of action, as her mom had been. I'm thankful to them for their strength and determination. FFFF has its place in our lives, to be sure. But as my mother's life shows—and mine too—when trauma is hidden by our reactions and left unexamined, it can rule our lives, determine our behavior, deepen its devastation, and become transgenerational.

EXERCISE

Reverse FFFF by Slow, Deep Breathing

What's your go-to FFFF mode: fight, flight, freeze, or faint? Next time you find yourself reacting or overreacting, I invite you to try to notice and interrupt the pattern. Stopping FFFF in the moment isn't hard. But it does take self-awareness. Here's what to do:

- *Step one:* Identify your FFFF pattern. When you are in a moment of calm, think about how you typically react when you feel threatened physically or emotionally. Do you become angry (fight)? Want to get away from it fast or ignore it (flight)? Or do you become paralyzed by it, unable to make a decision or take any action (freeze or faint)?
- *Step two:* Attune to yourself. The next time you feel your automatic reaction coming on, try to pause your thinking. Take a slow, deep breath. Then, slowly exhale.
- *Step three:* Breathe deeply some more. Very slowly, inhale and exhale over and over for a couple minutes. Notice as your heart rate slows to match your breathing. Notice your anxiety decreasing, and your ability to think and choose your actions increasing.

To reinforce this feeling and your ability to control your reactions, consider turning this breathing into a daily practice. To do that:

- *Step one:* For one minute a day, close your eyes and take a slow, deep breath. Then slowly exhale.
- *Step two:* Do it again. But this time, try to take only three to six breaths over one minute.
- *Step three:* Tell yourself "Good job. You did it." This will make your brain release dopamine, make you feel good, and make you more likely to keep up the practice of slow breathing.

This simple practice packs some powerful benefits. It gives your body a break from FFFF and all the cortisol that keeps you on edge. You feel better. You're more attuned to yourself. And over time, it will create a place within you where you can go for rest, relaxation, and self-comfort.

Chapter 4

WHY DOES THIS KEEP HAPPENING TO ME?

I can't say enough about how damaging secrets are to mental health. They keep us in a state of anxiety—always afraid we'll be exposed. They allow immature, unprocessed thoughts to grow into harmful misbeliefs we then use to make the decisions that shape our lives. When those secrets are about abuse, they also leave us more vulnerable to future abuse—a phenomenon not commonly acknowledged but commonly experienced.

"Why does this keep happening to me?" is a question I hear repeatedly from clients who've experienced sexual abuse. It's a question I asked myself many times over as well.

AGAIN

When I was eight (just two years after my first assault), my mom often took me along when she'd visit her friend—a German woman who, like Mom, married an American GI after the war and moved to Hawaii. "Auntie," as I called her, had an eleven-year-old son. The boy and I were always left alone to play while our moms drank coffee, smoked cigarettes, and talked stories.

His idea of "play," however, was a game of "if you show me yours, I'll show you mine." And without question, without pause, I showed him mine and then some—whatever he wanted, which was mostly a closer look or a touch sometimes. I didn't like it. But I also couldn't find it in myself to muster a "no."

Legally, what he did to me was not sexual assault because our age difference was three years and not five. Technically, I seemed like a willing participant, though I didn't say a word, didn't actively participate, and certainly never asked to "see his." At eleven, he too was a child and at an age where he was sexually curious and probably not seeking or getting answers from the adults in his life.

After each incident, I always blamed myself. I'd feel ashamed. I couldn't understand why I did the things I did. I wondered what was wrong with me. But then I'd let him do it again the next time.

I remember the day this boy and I were caught in the act. We were in his closet, and I was lying on my stomach with my pants down, my naked body exposed. All of a sudden it got quiet and still. I turned around and saw Auntie looking at us. Her son was sitting with his head down, looking dejected and limp. I remember Auntie said sternly, "Wash your hands!"

When my mom and I got home, I felt scared. I didn't know what she was going to do. She called me outside to sit with her on our brick wall. She'd never called me outside to talk before. We usually sat in the kitchen. So this made me think the situation was extra serious—and not to be overheard by others.

"Whose idea was it?" she asked.

"It was his."

"He says it was yours."

"No, it was his idea."

That was it. No more discussion. And we never talked about it again.

Once again, I was left alone to figure out this adult situation and put it into some kind of context for my brain. I had so many questions: What did my mom think of the situation? What did she think of me? What did she want me to do? What should I have done? Was I bad? Did she still love me? I didn't know. Maybe it was my fault. Did I somehow invite him to do that to me, without realizing it? I couldn't remember.

I had to admit that part of me felt relieved we'd been caught. At least I didn't have to play with him anymore. Or so I thought.

But when Auntie and Mom decided to get together at our house, Auntie arrived with her son. To my shock, they told us to go to my room and play together—alone! As the two women sat in the kitchen drinking coffee and smoking cigarettes, he molested me again. And I let him again. On some level, I thought maybe my mom was okay with it, which only added to my disempowerment and confusion.

Obviously, Auntie's talk with him had been as insubstantial as my mother's with me. I doubt she explained what he was feeling with puberty just around the corner and why. She hadn't helped him to find healthier, more appropriate ways to manage and express his natural curiosity and budding sexuality.

AND AGAIN

Unfortunately, that wouldn't be my last childhood assault. A few years later, the summer between sixth and seventh grade, my mom told me I was going to Europe. She said her cousin had invited me to travel with her family through France, Switzerland, Czechoslovakia, and Germany. She was excited for me. She told me this was a wonderful opportunity.

All I wanted in life was to please my mother. So, part of me was excited to go. But a bigger part of me didn't want to travel to Europe or anywhere with a family I'd never met. Again, if Mom had been attuned to me even a little bit, she'd have seen my trust issues and felt my fear. She'd have known I wasn't a kid looking for a trip to Europe with people I didn't know.

But off I went by myself at age eleven. I was greeted at the airport by my mom's cousin, her husband, and their children—a boy, Franz, who was fourteen; and a girl, Greta, who was eight. (I've changed their names here.) Both the dad and Franz spoke English.

Franz was cute. He had long brown hair and wore hippie jewelry. He was nice to me, always patiently interpreting for his mom and sister.

As we went from country to country, he explained the different foods and cultures to me.

After a couple of weeks, Franz began telling me he liked me. He also began asking me questions about boys in America. He asked whether I had a boyfriend and if I'd been kissed. Being eleven, I had a huge crush on Donny Osmond, David Cassidy, and a couple of boys in my class, but these were young-girl crushes. Franz asked me all kinds of questions about who I liked and if I liked him. His questions made me quiet.

Soon, he began coming into my room at night. He would lie next to me and kiss me. I remember feeling suffocated when he kissed me. Eventually, he went further and penetrated me with his fingers. He asked me whether I'd started my monthly bleeding. He said he was afraid I'd get a baby inside me. What he really wanted was to determine his risk should he escalate the assault.

I hadn't started menstruating yet. I'd learned about it in fifth-grade health class, but I didn't know about sexual intercourse. I also didn't know how I could get pregnant. Thankfully, I remained quiet and didn't answer.

He told me not to tell anyone about our secret love. A part of me liked being loved in this secret way. But another part of me felt awkward about it all. I felt what we were doing was wrong and that I wasn't the good girl people thought I was.

I never told anyone. I came home from Europe all smiles with memories of a lifetime to please my mother and with another shameful secret to tuck away in the back of my mind.

DISSOCIATION MAKES US EASY PREY

Notice in both of the above assaults, I was quiet and compliant—just as I had been the first time I was attacked. What made me—and what makes all sexual assault survivors—susceptible to repeated attacks is that we typically dissociate while it's happening. Meaning our brains disconnect from the event. We're not present in the situation. The FFFF response takes over and controls our reactions.

For example, people often dissociate during bad car accidents. After a crash, they can remember they were in a car and where they were going. But they cannot recall the moment of impact or injury. It's our brain's way of keeping us from experiencing an event it judges to be so painful and frightening it might throw us into shock.

After an assault, when our neocortex turns back on, we're likely to remember just enough to feel guilty without really knowing why. After repeated attacks, like most brains, my brain looked for a pattern to explain why this kept happening. But the only common denominator my innocent, inexperienced brain could find was me. So, that's where it put the blame. I told myself something must be inherently wrong with me, and worse, that I invited the repeated abuse.

It's also worth noting that the severity of the threat didn't matter to my brain. I reacted much the same when the threat was a sexually curious, confused eleven-year-old boy, as I did when it was a sexually deviant fourteen-year-old cousin. In neither instance did I have the presence to weigh the danger, my options, or my desires in the moment. I dissociated and my brain went right for my default response—freeze. In both instances, all I could be was an obedient robot. The thought of saying "no" never entered my mind. Because it couldn't. Dissociation and FFFF left me unable to think for myself, unable to say "no," and unable to get out of the situation.

The brain's survival mechanisms are powerful. They only grow stronger with each experience. Dissociation can be beneficial when memories of a horrific event serve no purpose. But when the event is a sexual assault, those memories and details are needed so they can be processed and brought to awareness. They allow an individual to stop being triggered, to re-establish autonomy, and to gain the ability to make deliberate, healthier choices.

AS FOR MOM AND AUNTIE

When I think about Mom and Auntie now allowing that boy and me to be alone again after having caught us in the act, I think that Auntie probably had a lot of the same issues as my mom. Having been teenagers in Europe during and after World War II, they probably shared the triggers of rape and sexual assault. Sex was too painful a subject to deal with—let alone sex and their prepubescent children. So when they found us "experimenting" in the closet, perhaps they both dissociated, and that's why they didn't get angry, offer any real guidance, or prevent it from happening again.

I'm sure that their inability to talk through the closet incident left that boy as confused as I was. Their relative silence provided the boy not only with another opportunity to molest me, but perhaps with the same idea I'd had—that our mothers thought it was okay. That this must be the way to behave. Not the healthiest way to send your children into puberty.

Auntie and her son may not have known my history of assault, but my mother did. And still, she was so damaged by her own trauma that she was incapable of seeing that I needed protection in that moment. She couldn't take my perspective into account. She could see the world only through her lens. And her brain was hijacked into protecting her.

Perhaps she comforted herself in the belief that, if it were really that bad, I'd have said "no"—as she liked to think she would have done. But if she'd really seen me for who I was and been able to attune to me, she would have seen I wasn't a child who had the wherewithal to say "no"—not before the assaults and most certainly not afterward.

ATTUNING TO OURSELVES

In therapy, I learned that it wasn't likely my mom would ever be able to attune to me—to overcome her own triggers to help me repair mine. I learned that my recovery depended on me being able to attune to myself.

To heal my pain and come to terms with my assaults, I had to get to know myself, physically and emotionally. This was vital information I didn't have. I'd never asked the simple question: Who am I? I'd always adopted the identities others had given me.

As a child, I was whoever my mom wanted me to be. A good girl. As much like her as I could will myself to be.

Later as a Christian, I found my identity in Jesus, my preachers, and the women in my church. They told me what to think, what to like and dislike, what to feel (though I had a lot of trouble feeling it), and what to aim for in life (a Christian husband and children).

And then as a Christian wife and mother, I allowed the church to further define me. I not only allowed but expected my husband to set the expectations for our lives—which put a lot of pressure on him. And I rode the wave of motherhood, focusing on my relationship with God first (as the church commanded). I had faith that my children would follow in my footsteps—which they did not. (Needless to say, I wasn't a very attuned parent myself during their childhoods.)

When I finally got to therapy, in order to heal from PTSD and a lifetime of secrets, I had to come out from behind all those assigned identities. I had to become myself. This would not be a fast journey. Indeed, it's a journey I'm still on. However, it's been my experience that the sooner you begin it, the sooner you stop living with the blame and shame of your traumas, gain control of your triggers, take back your life, and become far less likely to fall victim to any abuser of any kind ever again.

EXERCISE

Attune to Yourself

Attunement starts with a little curiosity. What am I feeling? Baby steps. Like when you're getting to know a new friend, you begin by talking with each other. Except in this exercise, you're having a conversation with yourself, between your mind and your physical body.

- *Step one:* Close your eyes and take a few deep breaths. Feeling your body move up and down, and in and out as you breathe.
- *Step two:* After a minute, ask your body, "How are you feeling today?" Then wait for your body's response. Wait a full minute. Your body will answer your question with physical sensations such as tightness in your back, tingling in your hands, or growling in your stomach.
- *Step three:* After another minute or two, respond to your body by saying, "Okay, thank you for telling me that I feel tightness in my chest, tingling in my hands, and hunger in my stomach."

Congratulations. You have just attuned to your physical body. Add this to your daily practices, and you'll get to know who you are from the inside out.

Chapter 5

LOST CONNECTION

When parents are consistently unable to attune to their child, the bond or connection between parent and child can develop in ways that make it difficult for the child to be resilient and manage traumas. Because our very survival as infants depends on our parent or primary caregiver, that relationship makes a huge impression on us. So the quality of it is important. It lays the groundwork for what we expect from and how we behave in other relationships—including, and most especially, in our relationship with ourselves.

In psychology, the bond or connection between two people is known as "attachment." British psychoanalyst John Bowlby coined the term while studying aspects of the mother-child bond on human development. Developmental psychologist Mary Ainsworth, who studied under Bowlby, built on his "attachment theory" and defined three attachment styles: secure, avoidant, and anxious. Later, psychologists Mary Main, who studied under Mary Ainsworth, and Judith Solomon would add a fourth: disorganized.

Your attachment style was created in your first three years of life, when you were pre-verbal. It was formed when you felt scared or stressed and had to figure out how to stay in the closest proximity possible to your primary caregiver to relieve that stress.

SECURE, AVOIDANT, ANXIOUS, DISORGANIZED

- A secure attachment pattern is created when an infant is cared for by an attentive parent who is reliable and emotionally available. These children learn they can trust in other people and the world. Securely attached babies tend to grow into adults with the self-love and confidence needed to engage in healthy relationships, as well as navigate disappointment and tragedy.
- An avoidant attachment pattern occurs when a child's primary caregiver is consistently unavailable emotionally. Such children resort to suppressing their feelings. They idealize their parents and their childhoods. They often describe their upbringing in vague terms like "great" and "can't complain." Not surprisingly, they grow into highly independent adults—with big trust issues when it comes to people and the world in general. Yet, they're conflicted. They feel intense loneliness but are never fully able to invest themselves in relationships.
- The anxious attachment pattern results from parents being inconsistent with care or very conditional with their love. These children blame themselves when their parents are neglectful. They take it upon themselves to win back their parents' love and attention. These children grow up with self-esteem issues. They go into adult relationships with a great need for love and a greater fear of abandonment. When negative things happen in their lives, they head straight to self-blame, where they don't usually find a healthy solution or resilience.
- The disorganized attachment pattern typically results from extreme trauma, abuse, and/or abandonment by parents or a primary caregiver. All children are born with a strong drive to connect with their caregiver. So when a caregiver becomes a threat to a child's survival, it confuses the child's brain. This can result in a disorganized attachment pattern. For these children, relationships become triggers causing them to dissociate and go into

FFFF. They can become anti-social. Some fail to develop empathy and grow up to be abusers themselves.

These are not strict categories. We tend toward one pattern over another and at various intensities. Unless you're one hundred percent securely attached (and that's rare), your attachment issues present themselves on a spectrum of skewed behaviors and subpar life-management skills. Bursts of anger, addiction, immaturity, inability to maintain relationships, inability to leave harmful relationships, and a susceptibility to PTSD are all clues an attachment pattern needs healing. If left unattended, these damaging behaviors follow us through childhood into our romantic relationships, and, finally, into our relationship with our children, affecting the quality of their attachment.

A CASE IN POINT: MY DAD

Unlike Mom, Dad barely talked at all. He never spoke about his childhood...ever. And I rarely asked. But one evening when I was about ten, I was sitting in our living room, where he was eating his dinner. As he watched TV, I watched him. In a matter of minutes, he'd gobbled down a plate piled high with rice, squash, pork, and kimchi. He inhaled it so fast, I wondered how he could eat like that without choking.

So without thinking, I asked, "Dad, why do you eat so fast?"

He looked at me for a full ten seconds.

Then he smiled, and answered, "Well, when I lived in the orphanage, all the children would sit in a circle. The food was placed in the middle in big, communal bowls. We all had to eat from the bowls. So whoever ate fastest got to eat more food."

Though I've thought about his answer so many times as an adult, I didn't give it much thought back then. I was probably astounded that he answered at all.

My dad was born in Hawaii, the fourth child of immigrant parents from Okinawa, Japan. His father was an alcoholic who spent all his money on booze, and came and went as he pleased. His mother had been a mail-order bride. They had four children: Seiko, Bea, Seiyo, and my dad, Seiden.

After my dad was born, his father deserted the family for good, leaving them penniless. His mother had a severe mental breakdown and was put in an asylum. Only five years old, with no one to care for him, my father was packed off to an orphanage without his siblings. Five years later, as soon as his brother Seiko was old enough, he got my dad out of the orphanage and raised him.

I only know these few details about my dad's family because my mother told me. And she only knew because my dad's siblings told her. In fact, in Germany, my dad told my mom that his mother was dead. Then, after my parents had been in Hawaii a few years, one night his brother, Seiyo, casually mentioned he was going to visit their mother.

"What! She's alive?" my mother asked. "I'm coming with you." If my mom was upset that her husband had lied to her for years, she never made that part of her story.

My mom said that when she and Seiyo entered my grandmother's room at the psychiatric hospital, my grandmother didn't acknowledge them. She sat silent and dull-eyed, staring forward. My mother described her as a porcelain geisha doll, locked inside herself, a shell of a person, physically alive but mentally dead.

Like his mother, my dad's silence kept him locked inside himself too.

When I was fifteen, Dad had a complete psychotic break. He was diagnosed with schizophrenia and hospitalized for months.

When he came home from the hospital, he had great difficulty with verbal utterances. Without warning, a guttural sound would rumble through his body and pop out his mouth. Shocked and embarrassed by the noise, he'd jump up, cover his mouth, and run to his room. Still, I could hear him behind his closed door, trying to stifle these unwanted and uncontrollable utterances.

Of course, neither he nor my mother explained what was going on to us children. Medically, he was diagnosed with Tourette syndrome.

His utterances were deemed a tic—an involuntary, repetitive vocalization or movement. But energetically, maybe even spiritually, I think it was my father's voice, tired of suppression and struggling to be heard.

It would be a year before my dad was able to return to work. But he did return.

HEALING IS ON A SPECTRUM TOO

My dad likely had a disorganized attachment pattern. The trauma and abandonment of his early years left him unable to form and participate in healthy relationships. But unlike his own father and mother, my dad didn't allow his inability to connect to completely void the relationships he did have. Perhaps his brother having rescued him and given him a home provided my dad with a little more security than either of his parents had known.

Though he was unable to attune or even really talk to any of us, my dad got up every morning at the crack of dawn and drove to McDonnell Douglas in Torrance, where he worked as a maintenance electrician. He arrived home every evening like clockwork. Then ate his dinner, worked in his garden, watched TV, and went to bed.

In other words, my dad provided. He didn't abandon.

His kids would never end up in an orphanage as he did. He even took my mother back and made the family whole again after she divorced him. It would take me years in therapy to appreciate what a mighty struggle this must have been for him and to acknowledge his success.

I'm sure the routine of work and his strict regimen after work provided needed structure to his disorganized mind. His quietness and self-isolation also helped him keep calm. And as so many with insecure attachment patterns do—as every member of my family eventually did, for better and worse—he created his own secure relationship with Jesus. A relationship with lots of rules and rituals to contain it. A relationship he would become more and more dependent on as he aged.

As long as I can remember, I always felt slightly afraid of my dad. He never hit me or yelled at me. But he never hugged me either. Or kissed me on the forehead, like TV dads do.

Still, I felt loved by him. He always changed the oil in my car and made sure my tires had enough pressure. When I broke down on the freeway, I called him for help because I knew he'd drop everything and come right away. When I needed money for college, Dad gave it to me, not Mom. I knew I could count on him in any situation. While he may never have won "Parent of the Year," his actions demonstrate an attempt at creating a positive attachment between us.

Once my dad retired at age seventy-seven, his Alzheimer's disease progressed quickly. In my whole life, the only emotion I ever witnessed my dad express was anger (mostly at Mom, but also at my brothers). Yet, once the Alzheimer's had taken hold, he became kind.

When I visited him at his care facility, he'd smile—something I'd rarely seen him do. And sometimes he'd say, "I know I've done something bad, but I can't remember what I've done. I'm sorry." Then he'd cry. It was heartbreaking. Yet, oddly, that vulnerability made him accessible to me. I had empathy for him and felt connection to him. I like to believe that the smiling man is who my dad really was—and would have become—before life's traumas shaped him. He died at the age of eighty-five.

As sad as it is to think about, I now understand why he never said the words "I love you" to me or anyone. His bridge of connection to the world and to other human beings was missing. He couldn't trust his inner guide, so he structured his life through routines and religion, and built the best attachments he could.

TRANSGENERATIONAL BROKENNESS

My dad's attachment pattern did affect me. Temperamentally, I was quiet like him. I retreated from life. And I struggled to form relationships—though unlike my dad, I very consciously craved them. When I was too quiet—which was often—my mother would complain, "You're just like your dad. You don't say anything." She was right.

But it would be my mother and her own attachment issues that would have more influence on my attachment pattern. She was, after all, my primary caregiver, the person I looked to for survival.

From her stories, I know that she and her mother were close. I also know that her mother made the rules and ran the show—no questions asked. My mom didn't make a decision for herself, my grandmother made them. Perhaps that's because it's the only way my grandmother knew to maintain order in a home with nine children and an emotionally distant father.

Like her mother, my mom also married an emotionally distant man under duress. (A relationship pattern I continued, minus the duress part.) She too parented as a total dictator, never to be questioned. This was especially true when it came to me, her constant companion. She directed my every move. She told me what I liked and what I didn't, what to do and how to do it. She set the expectations for my life, and I tried to oblige. I often felt I fell short—and she allowed me to feel that way.

All that, combined with her volatile temper, kept me on my toes as a child. One minute she was delighting in having me by her side, the next she'd explode in anger because she didn't like what I was wearing (which in all probability, she'd picked out). As a child, I was never sure which mom I was going to get. I was never sure if I was going to please her or make her mad. So I was constantly monitoring her moods. Figuring out what to do. Trying to manage everything and everyone in the house. There was no room to develop a sense of self. But what did develop was an anxious attachment pattern. I had a deep need to be accepted and a palpable fear of making a mistake.

This made it very difficult for me to be in a relationship, even friendships. I'd watch the pretty girls talking and laughing with each other. I wished so hard I could join them. But then when they'd invite me over, I'd become so self-conscious that I'd make an excuse and decline their invitation. When the neighborhood kids gathered casually to play a pickup game or hang out, I never went.

Years later in therapy when I looked at this behavior pattern closely,

I learned what prevented me from joining in with other kids: I didn't know who to be. More to the point, I didn't know who they wanted me to be. If they could have just let me know, I could have become that person. I did it for my mom all the time. But to show up as myself, I was at a loss. I didn't know who that was.

After I was sexually assaulted, my anxious attachment style ensured I would put my mother's feelings before my own, because I had no "me" to consider. Instead of crying or clinging to her (as a normal six-year-old might), I fell into my pattern and did what I thought would make her comfortable. I stayed quiet and compliant. I did what I was told. Keeping my questions, my feelings, my terror tucked deep inside resulted in PTSD. It also laid the groundwork for the two subsequent assaults to occur.

TRANSGENERATIONAL HEALING

I lived my life in my head with my own doubts and fears, with my longings and fantasies constantly swirling around and never being expressed, just like my dad. Also like my dad, I eventually found a workaround for relationships, so at least I appeared normal. I too formed relationships through doing. As a teenager, I played on the tennis team and was active in my church. In college, I went to parties and drank. When I got older, I got more into church, specifically women's Bible studies.

But I never made real friends. I had put up walls of protection that I was not aware of. I think to really connect with someone, you need to feel securely attached within yourself. You need to feel comfortable being yourself. I was neither. When I tried to connect and make friends, my discomfort would cause both me and the other person to move away from each other.

But once in therapy, I started to learn the value of putting myself first. Which demanded that I come to know a "me" to put first. That meant repairing my attachment style, which gave me the tools and support to connect to the real "me."

Securely attached parents naturally behave in ways with their children that transfer their inner security without consciously thinking about it. In their own individual ways, my father and mother did all they knew to do to keep us safe and give us the best life. Yet, no deed my father could have done or rule my mother could have made would have kept me safe from that first assault. A more secure attachment pattern, however, would have seen us all through the initial trauma and saved me from PTSD.

Secure attachment was not a life skill my parents had to give. So I would eventually have to develop it for myself—with the added incentive of being able to model it for my own children.

EXERCISE

The Body Scan

Children learn how to feel their feelings through a psychological process called "reflection." That's when parents "reflect" back to the child what they're feeling by validating the child's feelings. For example, when I felt happy baking cookies with my mom, she'd smiled at me and say, "I can see you're really enjoying baking cookies with me." I learned what happiness felt like in my body.

When it comes to more difficult emotions (the ones people don't like to talk about), we, as children, don't get as much reflection. So we often become detached from how those emotions feel in our bodies.

An exercise called The Body Scan can help us reattach to those emotions and ourselves. In this exercise, you reflect back to yourself what you're feeling by becoming familiar with the sensations in your body. You'll need about thirty minutes to be alone in a place where you can sit in silence.

- *Step one:* Sit in a chair with your feet flat on the floor, your hands on your knees. Close your eyes and feel your breathing for two to three minutes.
- *Step two:* Feel your body fill up and expand when you inhale, and feel your body relax, settle down, and release your breath when you exhale.
- *Step three:* After a couple of minutes, you will become aware of what's going on inside of your body and are ready to scan.
- *Step four:* Start with your feet. Look for sensations such as the contact points on the bottom of your feet to the ground. Do you feel the contact points where your shoes touch your feet, the pressure points? Do your feet feel hot, warm, or cold? Do your feet feel sweaty? Do your feet feel stiff? Do your feet feel any tightness or pain? Do you feel any energy or electricity shocks in your feet? Can you feel any tingling or movement inside of your feet? Perhaps pulsing, twitching, or itching? Your goal is to sit with and notice any and all sensations that arise from your body.
- *Step five:* Move up to your lower legs and ask those same questions. What sensations do you feel in your lower legs?
- *Step six:* Then move your attention into your upper legs. And ask the same questions.
- *Step seven:* Keep moving your attention slowly up your body into your abdomen, chest, back, arms, neck, shoulders, and head. Take your time, and notice the sensations by observing and investigating. Receive information about your body by feeling the sensations that arise.

As this becomes a regular practice, you'll become more and more comfortable with both your body and your feelings. You'll come to accept yourself—all of you.

Chapter 6

FALSE PROPHETS

I don't remember the exact moment or even the year it happened. I know I was around thirteen. I remember it happening suddenly. One day we were a sad, lonely, angry, lost family, and the next, Jesus touched our hearts, and voila!—we were saved, found, forgiven, and happy. To me, my family's conversion to Christianity produced the miracle I'd longed for.

My sister Sadie converted first. She said Jesus appeared to her when she was in the hospital temporarily paralyzed with a broken back. He spoke to her and then came into her heart. After that, she started attending a charismatic, new-agey kind of evangelical church that belonged to the fast-growing Calvary Chapel sect of Christianity—a sect founded in Southern California by hippies who'd grown tired of sex, drugs, and rock 'n roll. Their sermons and music were emotional, upbeat, and modern—so they attracted a younger crowd. Sadie's life changed overnight. She transformed from a drug-and-alcohol-using bohemian into a godly young woman.

One Sunday, Sadie invited us all to go to church with her. From that day forward, we were Christians. We joined the church. Joined the choir. Joined the Bible study groups. We even joined the church's bowling league. We'd never had a religion before. But having this one now, we became a happy family for the first time.

My mom might have been the happiest of all—and that's what mattered most to me. Her Bible now joined her other permanent fixtures—ashtray, cigarettes, and lighter—on the kitchen counter, where she and I sat most days to talk. And now, along with her World War II stories, she'd tell me what God had told her heart through the pastor's sermon that week. Often, his sermons had a lot to do with God rescuing His people from pain. A theme she especially loved because it gave new meaning and purpose to her war stories.

"God is so good. He gave me power to escape the Russian Zone," she'd say. It gave her comfort that her suffering had not been in vain and that God had a plan for our lives—for her life.

The Bible made so much sense when Mom explained it.

"Why are we to fear the Lord?" I asked once.

"It doesn't mean to be scared of God, but to respect His power and His greatness," she said in a calm, sure voice.

I nodded my head and smiled. But inside I was thinking, "I hope He doesn't make me suffer too much for His glory. What will I do if He makes me suffer?" I also worried a lot about what might happen if I needed to be disciplined by an almighty, all-powerful, righteous, and holy God.

But my little worries about God's judgment were a small price to pay for the difference He was making in our family. This "God takes away His people's pain" theme was working for all of us. Our lives shifted. Not only did we go to church three and sometimes four days out of the week, but my parents stopped fighting and yelling. Jesus had changed them. We had friends. We went to fun activities—church parties, church sports events, and church retreats. I stopped worrying about my parents' unpredictable anger. I was less afraid, less on edge.

The church community provided a place where my family and I felt connected, safe, and supported—instantly and in spades. Our lives were great now, thanks to God. And I loved Him for it.

CHRISTIAN SOLDIERS

Our church taught that sin was the problem and Jesus, the solution.

Simple, right? Obey His law, and we'd be on the road to a good life. Admit we were sinners, repent, and do better. We could do that. Jesus had the power to save us. Jesus had power to heal us. All we had to do was believe and allow Jesus to lead us. If a feeling, experience, thought, or teaching from our past countered or threatened that faith, we were to put it out of our mind and let Jesus take the wheel.

This forward-focused doctrine offered my parents a lovely solution to all their problems. The key tenet being that once you had this belief in God, the sins of your past were forgiven, and you never had to think about them again. My siblings too were happy to leave our angry upbringing behind and focus on the promise of a brighter future. And I no longer had to struggle with my past sexual abuse. Every member of the family turned everything over to Jesus. All our mistakes and pain, all our traumas were suddenly and miraculously washed away in the blood of Jesus. We were Christian soldiers. And just like the hymn said, my family was marching "onward"—not backward.

As part of their newfound, forward-looking, Christian worldview, Mom and Dad both decided to follow the "Wealth and Prosperity Gospel." This gospel taught that God wanted us to be healthy, wealthy, and wise. And we achieved that through positive thought. The harder life got, the more positive God commanded us to be.

"Speak the truth and don't be shy about it," Mom would tell me. Yet, neither she nor the Wealth and Prosperity Gospel said what to do if the truth was negative. She was so sure God was real and that he'd healed her, made her whole—mind, body, and spirit. Mom came to believe that people who weren't healed or whole (i.e. people who had problems) either didn't have enough faith in God or were disobedient to God.

I wanted more than anything to have faith, to be obedient, and to believe like Mom.

TREATING A MENTAL PROBLEM WITH A SPIRITUAL SOLUTION

When in emotional pain, people often look to outside forces to take the pain away. It's easier than looking inward and facing the reality of what's happened. But outward fixes (religions, drugs, work, unhealthy relationships) only serve to mask our trauma; they provide only temporary relief. They can't heal trauma, make it go away, or restore real function to a person or a family.

Think of my family as a building with four walls. Before we found Jesus, we were all leaning on each other trying to keep our building upright and intact. But with each of us being emotionally insecure, every wall was wobbly, the foundation was insecure, and so the building wasn't strong.

Under increasing stress—my parents' constant fighting, the divorce and remarriage, my sexual assault, my siblings becoming teenagers—our walls were about to fall over when God came into the picture. Psychologically, we each needed to face our past, work through it, and process our trauma. Through that work, each of us would have developed a secure inner foundation and a secure sense of self, allowing us to stand sure-footed and relate to one another by sharing our feelings, needs, and thoughts openly and independently. But that wasn't going to happen in Middle America in 1973. Religion was much more accessible and acceptable, and seemed to do the trick. No uncomfortable introspection required.

The church shored up our foundation just enough to keep us standing. God commanded us to keep our eyes on Jesus and the future. Because if we looked back, that meant we didn't think Jesus' sacrificial death was powerful enough to absolve our past sins. Remember Lot's wife? She looked back, against God's warning, and was turned into a pillar of salt.

I'm not saying religion is false. Seeking God, the divine, or a higher power is found in every culture. Religions around the world bring meaning, guidance, social support, and great comfort to people's lives.

What I'm saying is that my family's approach to and use of religion was false. Expecting it to instantaneously cure our deep psychological wounds was wrong.

It's no wonder that the sect we chose was irresistible. It forbid us to look at what we each feared most—our past. It encouraged us not to think for ourselves—in fact, not to think at all, which was such a relief. All we had to do was believe in the supernatural mystery of the trinity—Father, Son, and Holy Ghost—to take away all troubles, love us unconditionally, punish us when we disobeyed, and set us on a righteous path. All of this seemed like a soothing balm to my family.

For the first time in my life, we were accepted into a wonderful community of people who were looking to be better in life. We also became closer as a family, but only because my mom and dad put a religious Band-Aid over their own relationship and their relationships with my sister and older brother.

It's no wonder I happily gave myself over to whatever power caused this "miracle." With all my heart, I wanted to believe that Jesus had healed my family's past sins, mine included. Even better, anything that might haunt us in the future could now be categorized as a sin and be forgiven. All we had to do was repent and forgiveness was guaranteed with God.

Reconciling our trauma, on the other hand, with self-exploration was so much more complicated and painful. And there were no guarantees.

I wanted a guarantee, and Christianity delivered.

DOUBTING DOROTHY

No matter how much I wanted that guarantee, however, I never was a hundred percent sure that my sins were forgiven. No matter how hard I prayed, no matter how hard I tried to force the feelings. I just didn't feel Him. Of course, I blamed myself for this, not God. I thought something must be wrong with me—my go-to conclusion and a typical one for someone with PTSD. I couldn't escape the suspicion that religion had only papered over my pain, and that my trauma was still there selecting my thoughts and driving my actions.

But I didn't know that then, so I adopted "fake it till you make it" as my plan. When I stood next to my mom in church, I'd peek out of my "closed" eyes to get a clue what to do with myself, what the right reaction would be to whatever was going on. If she had her eyes closed and was swaying to the music with her hands raised up to God, then I closed my eyes again, raised my hands in the air, and sang along. Mom always looked so in awe in church, caught up in heaven with Jesus. But when my mom would cry during the service, I couldn't mimic that. Man, what was wrong with me?

I'd peek out at the crowd periodically to make sure I was in sync with everyone. On stage, the cute, hip drummer's long, brown hair always swayed back and forth as he played. When he was overcome with love for Jesus, he'd stop drumming and raise his hands up to God. He looked angelic. I had a crush on him. He was quiet and always smiled because, as he told in his testimony, God had saved him from a life of drugs and misery. Just like He had with my sister.

I worried about my salvation. Everyone, it seemed, had a fantastic testimony about how they came to be saved. Jesus had healed their chronic pain. Or brought them back from the brink of suicide. Or saved them from the occult. And He always brought meaning and purpose to their lives that they hadn't known was possible. Even in the Bible, the stories of salvation were dramatic. Jesus met Saul on the road to Damascus, blinded him for three days. Afterward, he became the Apostle Paul who wrote most of the New Testament.

I'd watch my fellow churchgoers closely as they testified. They all expressed themselves so emotionally and with so much gratefulness.

My only testimony was that I was a sinner and asked Jesus to forgive me of my sins. That was it. No real story. No big deal. However, that didn't stop me from wanting something dramatic and emotional to happen to me too—so I could express it. A good story would be proof I was saved.

Adding to my distress, one Sunday the pastor said, "You can't get into heaven on your parents' coattails. Everyone must be accountable to God for their own sins, and you must accept Jesus personally into your heart. You must develop your own relationship with Jesus or when you get to heaven, Jesus will say, 'I never knew you. Cast this sinner into hell!'"

I'll never forget that sermon. As you might imagine, it scared the bajeebers out of me. I was absolutely counting on riding my mother's coattails (and my sister's too, if I had to) right on up to the pearly gates. So I prayed harder. I asked Jesus to forgive me of my sins and to come into my heart. I promised to give my life to Him and to follow Him faithfully forever.

I waited to feel something, but nothing dramatic happened to me.

SEX, THE CHURCH, AND SEXUAL TRAUMA

Outwardly, "faking it until making it" was working for me. I was happier than I'd ever been. I had clear directions for how to be a good girl, and I liked that. Even though I didn't have a great testimony, I was accepted by my fellow Christians. All I had to do was follow the rules—which I was good at.

So I put my doubts about myself where I put all my other inconvenient thoughts. I buried them in my brain and went to church.

As a good Christian, of course, my goal was to remain sexually pure until marriage. The Bible was clear on that. And since Jesus had already forgiven the sins of my childhood sexual abuse—which I still blamed myself for—I wasn't going to tempt fate. Also, as a young teen whose hormones had yet to appear, it didn't seem like a big ask.

Our church put a lot of emphasis on sexual sins. So I figured they were especially bad. God gave us a lot of instructions when it came to sex. It seemed there were rules for every sexual thought, desire, and behavior from adultery to fornication to homosexuality. Even the sexual sins of the mind, like lust and desire, were covered in detail. Sexual sins were directly linked to the body and the sinful human nature that opposed God's pureness. Sexual sins had the power to defile someone who was otherwise good.

Sunday after Sunday, we'd hear warning from the pulpit such as:
- Flee from sexual immorality.
- God will judge the adulterer and sexually immoral.
- But I will tell you that anyone who looks at a woman lustfully has already committed adultery with her in his heart.
- You shall not lie with a man as with a woman; it is an abomination.
- Do not be deceived: Neither the sexually immoral nor idolaters nor adulterer nor men who have sex with men nor thieves nor the greedy nor drunkards, nor slanderers nor swindlers will inherit the kingdom of God.
- Put to death therefore what is earthly, whatever belongs to your earthly nature: sexual immorality, impurity, lust, evil desire, and greed, which is idolatry.

We learned that as human beings we were incapable of controlling ourselves when it came to sex. We might try, but we'd fail. Jesus was our only hope.

Driving all this home for me, I witnessed a couple of big moral failures within our small church community. Our music pastor had to step down because he'd had an affair with a young, single woman in our church. And then, an older teenager who was a part of my group was kicked out of the church because she refused to stop sleeping with her boyfriend.

I felt embarrassed for both of them being so publicly shamed in front of the congregation. I remember the teenage girl sobbing loud and hard. Her body shook uncontrollably. I felt bad, but I didn't cry. Instead, I internalized the message that sexuality was a huge deal and a huge problem. And I never wanted to get caught and called out, ever.

Thankfully, there were the sermons just about every week that focused on God's solution for our sex problem. The solution was marriage. Sex, our pastor told us, was beautiful only between a husband and wife because it's an illustration of the relationship between Jesus and the Church.

That particular analogy was another mystery to me, but it seemed to make sense to the adults. The point was sex was for marriage. Period. No fooling around, not with another person, and definitely, not with yourself.

Unfortunately, during all this education, I was maturing into a full-fledged adolescent. As hard as I tried, I couldn't stop my body from growing up. My teen hormones kicked in, bringing on my body's natural sexual feelings and creating problems for me. I started having lustful thoughts that I couldn't control. My tried-and-true solution for complicated problems—repress, deny, bury—was failing me.

I tried to focus on something other than myself. But I now had this deviant mind (that I blamed Satan for) filling with sinful thoughts. I couldn't pretend this wasn't happening. I was dealing with a Heavenly Father who could read my mind. It was becoming impossible for me to be a good girl for God. I felt guilty all the time like I had before I knew Jesus. I was losing the sense of security I'd once gotten from church.

At the same time, and contrary to what God wanted for me, I wanted a boyfriend. I wanted what other girls had. I wanted to be liked by boys. I'd dream about it endlessly. But because my thoughts about my sexual abuse had not been resolved, when I fantasized about boys and sex, the neural pathway of my sexual abuse became wired to my feelings of sexual arousal in my brain. This added more guilt and shame to just thinking about, let alone acting on, my sexual desires.

And there was more.

Fantasizing about a secret sexual tryst produced a quick and easy sexual response that naturally called for release to alleviate the pressures and anxieties that all normal teenagers feel. Self-sexual release gave me a quick "feel good," which because of my Christian beliefs then led to my feeling very bad afterward. The Bible was clear: Masturbation was a bad, bad sin that would get me into lots of trouble with God.

So, I never told anyone. I simply spiraled within the cycle of shame and secrecy. It was my secret sin that I couldn't talk about, not even to God. (Though I knew He knew.)

BREAKING IN TWO

All that conflict was a lot for a naïve, confused adolescent girl to deal with on her own. My inability to reconcile my faith, my physical reality, and my past sexual abuse weighed heavily on me.

To manage the conflict inside my head, my brain chose to compartmentalize my thinking. Compartmentalization is a subconscious psychological defense mechanism that is used to deal with conflicting values, thoughts, emotions, and beliefs by keeping them in separate places in the mind.

It is similar in concept to dissociative identity disorder, which used to be called multiple personality disorder, in which separate personalities exist within one person's mind. I didn't develop distinct personalities but inside my head, there was Godly Dorothy and Deviant Dorothy. Godly Dorothy loved to pray and felt good doing it. I was taught that an important principle of prayer was to praise and thank God, to be grateful for all that He'd done for me. So, I'd thank Him for my family, my pastor, and my church. I'd thank Him for healing me. I'd thank Him for everything in my life that was good. Then, I'd feel good about myself because I'd pleased God. I'd feel connected to Him spiritually. Through prayer, I escaped the sinful natural world and my sinful natural body. I'd make His world, the spiritual world, my only world, at least for a little while.

Deviant Dorothy saw my struggles (as my church taught) as "spiritual warfare." Like Eve, I had allowed Satan to use my body's lustful desires against me. And yet, this was who I was. Or, maybe Satan was inside me? I secretly feared these sexual feelings were caused by my earlier sexual abuse—my "original sin"—making me act out with what I considered aberrant behaviors, though in truth they were all very normal behaviors for a teenage girl.

For instance, I couldn't stay away from juicy romance novels. Even though I knew it didn't please God and probably upset Him, I loved reading hot sex scenes. In my novels, the women were the heroes of the story. But they were sinful women. Worse, I wanted to be them. I wanted to be bad but at the same time was terribly afraid of being bad.

As Deviant Dorothy, I felt I couldn't control myself—just as my church had warned in so many sermons. My desires scared me. But I couldn't tell anyone. I couldn't ask anyone about it. I just kept smiling.

Without realizing it, I had developed a habit of smiling whenever I felt nervous, uncomfortable or conflicted—which was most of the time. Along with my shyness and quiet demeanor, that miscue distanced me further from people. When others don't know how you really feel, it makes it difficult for them to connect.

This cycle of incompatible desires, thoughts, and emotions played on a never-ending loop in my head. All these mental gymnastics only encouraged my growing PTSD. Paranoia, anxiety, and irrational thinking became my constant companions. In my mind, I "reasoned" that since God is perfect, I must be the problem. Something was wrong with me.

The real problem here was that my church's view of sexuality and the human condition in general were as immature as I was. They believed that sexuality and any deviation from their very strict rules around human relationships were caused by a supernatural force—"evil," as in "the devil made me do it." They led us to believe our mind and body were in constant conflict, a righteous battle, that only Jesus could resolve.

In Romans 7:15–20, the Apostle Paul confesses:

> [15] *I do not understand what I do. For what I want to do I do not do, but what I hate I do.* [16] *And if I do what I do not want to do, I agree that the law is good.* [17] *As it is, it is no longer I myself who do it, but it is sin living in me.* [18] *For I know that good itself does not dwell in me, that is, in my sinful nature. For I have the desire to do what is good, but I cannot carry it out.* [19] *For I do not do the good I want to do but the evil I do not want to do—this I keep on doing.* [20] *Now if I do what I do not want to do, it is no longer I who do it, but it is sin living in me that does it.*

If Paul had had a good therapist, he would have stopped the self-blaming and shaming, realized he had agency here, and taken an honest look at why he was saying one thing and doing another. Once he understood, he then could integrate his thoughts and deeds, and move forward in alignment with what he truly wanted in life.

To a traumatized person like me, my church's insistence on using supernatural forces (angels, devils, prophecies) to explain biological functions only served to cloud my already distorted vision of myself and sex—further disconnecting my brain from my body, disconnecting me from reality, and creating fertile ground for PTSD. Their message of lack of autonomy over my body—the devil pushing me one way, God pulling me another, and me a helpless pawn in the middle of this metaphysical battle—was especially harmful to a person who had been sexually assaulted; it only intensified my trauma.

What would have been healthier for me and all teenagers in my church would have been a celebration of this new phase of our lives—after all, it's about life. They could have provided us with teachings that explained what we were feeling, why we were feeling it, and how we might manage these new urges in ways that both honored ourselves and maybe even God.

But at that time, I believed my only way back to grace was to find a man and get married.

EXERCISE

Heart Breathing

Part of the reason it took me decades to recognize and deal with my childhood trauma was that I bypassed it successfully using spiritual practices. There's no end of ways to avoid dealing with our trauma. Some people become overly involved—busying themselves—with other people's problems, a.k.a. the Good Samaritan bypass. Still others use food, drugs, alcohol, shopping, movies, work—any substance or action that can distract them, keep them busy, and keep them from looking at what happened to them.

Though we might successfully distract our minds from trauma, it still resides in our bodies. It often reveals itself through chronic illness, pain, or disease. This is not to say that trauma causes disease. But the stress brought on by suppressing the trauma may aggravate a condition. The following is a partial list of chronic illnesses that might be negatively affected through unresolved childhood trauma. Circle the illnesses you suffer from and fill in others you may have that aren't listed.

Obesity
Diabetes
High Blood Pressure
Atherosclerosis
Migraines
Asthma
Arthritis
Irritable Bowel Syndrome
Gastroesophageal Reflux Disease (GERD)
Fibromyalgia
Back and Neck Pain
Eczema and Skin Rashes
Periodontal Disease
Chronic Fatigue Syndrome
Chronic Pain Syndrome
Other: _____

When you relieve stress, you create a more healing environment in your body. A technique called Heart Breathing can help you create that environment:

- *Step one:* Place one hand on your heart and the other hand on the area of pain in your body (if possible).
- *Step two:* Inhale slowly into your heart. Imagine filling all four chambers of your heart.
- *Step three:* Exhale slowly into your body's pain. Imagine sending heart breath from your heart into the area of your body that is suffering, i.e., your brain for migraines.
- *Step four:* Repeat steps two and three, three times.
- *Step five:* Continue to heart breathe and say aloud to the part of your body that is suffering:
    "I am here for you"
    "Your pain matters to me"
    "You are not alone. I am here with you"
    "I care about your pain"
- *Step six:* Repeat steps two and three again.
- *Step seven:* Journal about whatever came up for you.
    What did you feel?
    What did you notice?
    Did your pain increase or decrease?

This practice, of course, will not cure your disease. But by reducing your stress, you may reduce your pain and support your body in healing.

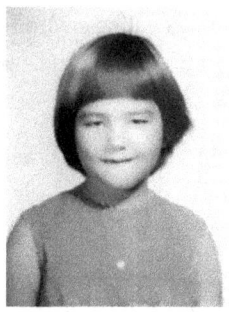

School picture of me at five or six years old

My seventh birthday. My sister, Sadie, is behind me. (Not sure who anyone else is.)

Me and Dad

Our wedding day

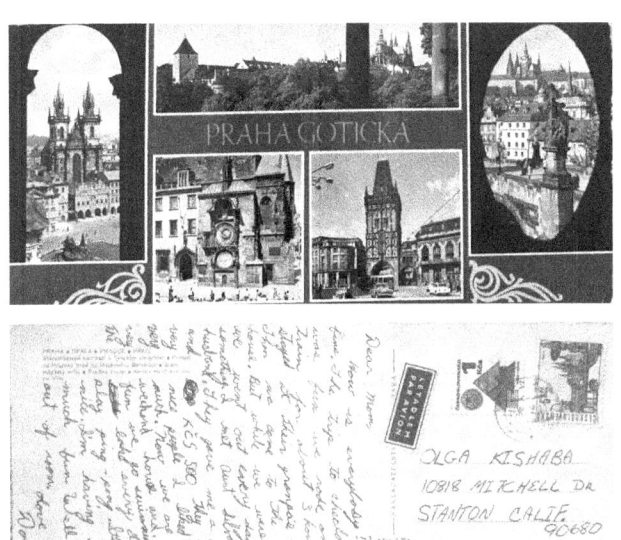

A postcard I sent to Mom when I visited her birthplace, Prague in 1972.

My mom with Emma and Dustin

Emma and Dustin, 2019

My granddaughter, Elena, learning to ride her bike

My brothers, Glenn and Owen; my sister, Sadie; and me standing by our mom's casket, 2017

My first-place win at a Toastmaster speech contest

Opening up my own practice as a mind-body psychotherapist

Jim and me, posing in our navy uniforms for our granddaughter's Veterans Day project, 2019

Jim and me, Christmas 2019

Chapter 7

A MATCH MADE IN TRAUMA

My church preached that the marriage relationship between a man and woman was the backbone of a moral society. Thus, married women had a higher value (in the church's eyes) than single women. Married women with children were even higher.

From my perspective, marriage was the ultimate blessed path in life. It's the path I chose to doggedly pursue after high school. My husband would be the spiritual leader of our home and the financial provider. Me, the good Christian wife, would be his helpmate.

In spite of my underlying doubts, I grew spiritually through my Bible studies. My body matured physically. But unprocessed trauma prevented me from growing up emotionally. Though I was preparing to head off to college, I remained as dependent on my mother as if I were six years old.

At seventeen, I happily allowed her to make all my decisions with little or no input from me. She still chose my clothes! I was little more than her mannequin when we shopped. She picked out what she thought would look best on me. Then I tried it on and waited for her opinion. I trusted that she knew better than I did. She also instructed me on how to walk and stand so the clothes would hang right.

My mother's trauma-fueled need for control and my trauma-fueled need to be controlled were a match made in heaven. Without a secure sense of myself, even if I had an opinion—which I didn't—I wouldn't have trusted my judgment enough to act on it.

What I did have was a strengthening dependent personality disorder to add to my bucket of emotional impairments stemming from unresolved trauma. I relied on my mother to meet all my emotional and physical needs. I feared being separated from her counsel. I had an insatiable thirst for her approval. All of which manifested in submissiveness and clingy behavior. Everyday decisions—what to wear, what to eat, whether or not to like a TV show or a book—were so impossible for me that I willingly handed over my life to her suggestions.

Though I never could have expressed it then, my focus on marriage as my one true goal almost certainly emanated from wanting to please my mother, and secondarily from my unspoken but desperate desire to remain dependent, to have someone else make the decisions—in short: to be taken care of. Marriage, as I saw it and as my church presented it, offered a socially and spiritually acceptable way for me to transition directly from my mom to a Christian husband.

Again, as with religion, it's not the institution of marriage that's bad here. Far from it, it can be (and has been for me) a wonderful way to go through life. What was unhealthy is the way I thought about marriage and needed to use it—as an escape from reality and an acceptable way to *not show up* in my own life.

THE HUNT IS ON

So I packed my Bible, my romance novels (!), my Christian albums, and my secular eight-track tapes, and headed off to college to find a Christian man to marry me.

What I found, instead, was that college required self-direction and self-motivation—two things Mom and Jesus hadn't prepared me for. The reading and homework quickly overwhelmed me. For the first time in my life, I got Cs, Ds, and even Fs on tests.

I also discovered secular friends, partying, and alcohol. All it took was a few drinks and my stress over a bad grade miraculously disappeared. And surprisingly, I liked my secular friends. I felt more relaxed around them. Maybe it was the beer, maybe it was the non-judgment. Who knows?

Once the buzz wore off, however, I was left with a lot of guilt. Guilt about drinking. Guilt about hanging out with people who weren't Christian. Guilt about not studying enough.

Luckily, as a Christian, I could rid myself of these feelings of guilt without really having to examine what was behind them. I didn't have to ask myself why I was drinking, why hanging out with non-Christians was a problem, and why I wasn't studying. Or what was driving my self-destructive behavior. I didn't have to find my own answers to any of that. All I had to do was trod off to a campus Bible study group, admit I was a sinner, and look to Jesus for forgiveness. I'd re-devote myself to God and my studies for as long as I could remain contrite. Then, I'd start the whole cycle over.

This how I limped through college.

As before, my brain compartmentalized. I had a black-and-white worldview, which was how I saw myself. Either I was good or bad, obedient or disobedient, faithful or unfaithful. Unlike most people between eighteen and twenty-two, I never developed a healthy, integrated, independent personality in college—because I didn't know what that was. I had no way to conceive that that was something I should aim for. Instead, I remained dependent upon God and my mom to tell me what to do and which direction to go.

My life—who I was, what I did, whom I befriended—was being defined by trauma. If something or someone didn't aid my survival, then my traumatized brain disregarded them. I didn't spend my time creating, exploring, discovering, or innovating in college, as most young adults do. I was way too busy trying to figure out what I needed to do and say in order to please other people—which made me a well-liked but a pretty uninteresting person, most especially to myself. I didn't know how to feel confident, worthy, or good enough. Trauma was turning me into "the invisible woman" who disappeared when faced with everyday problems.

After five years, I emerged from college with a bachelor's degree in biology—but no engagement ring.

RESCUE ON THE HIGH SEAS

Inevitably, people asked, "What's next for you, Dorothy?" I would get embarrassed. I didn't know. I had an okay job in a medical laboratory cleaning glassware. But here I was at twenty-three without a boyfriend, let alone a husband. I knew my mom was disappointed.

Though I didn't much go anywhere but work and church, and none of the single guys in either place showed any interest in me, I recommitted myself to my search for a Christian husband.

One day, a co-worker asked me if I wanted to join the U.S. Navy with her. "If we join together," she said, "we'd be put in the navy's buddy program." A ton of bricks lifted off my shoulders. She'd not only given me a direction in life, but joining the navy would allow me to run away from my mom's disappointment, from my dead-end job, from reminders of the careers my college friends were building.

The problem, of course, was I could not run away from myself. Wherever I went, there I'd be, as they say, along with my trauma and shame. The only escape from them would've been to face and process the trauma—and I wasn't that desperate yet.

After bootcamp and training, my friend and I were sent to Charleston, South Carolina, to serve aboard the USS Frank Cable, AS-40—a submarine tender, which is a supply-and-repair shop for attack submarines. When off-duty, I partied for the first few months on ship just to get along with everyone. Then, I felt the Holy Spirit (or more like the guilty spirit) overtake me. With the words "fear the Lord and repent" ringing in my head, I found a church service, went forward, and repented.

I probably would have followed the same survival cycle I'd used in college—rebel, repent, re-devote, repeat—but two weeks after that first atonement, I met Jim.

JIM

I'd heard rumors about a Jesus-freak sailor—Petty Officer First Class James Charles Husen Jr.—coming to my division for temporary duty. He was to teach sailors about nuclear radiation and how to stay safe working with radioactive materials. I was to assist him with the paperwork. Leader and helpmate right from the start—perfect for me!

On the day my new boss was to arrive, I looked up from my desk to see a young, blond-haired, blue-eyed man pop his head through the door. He was tall and slender and had a huge smile on his face.

"He's cute," I said to myself. "And a Christian to boot."

He looked so happy, kind, and good. "My mom would approve," I immediately thought.

I tried to be the best assistant I could; I completed all the tasks he gave me. He seemed pleased with my work. But he was nice to everyone. I couldn't tell if he really liked me.

I watched him like I used to watch my mom. Jim worked so hard that the other sailors complained about him. They made fun of him behind his back because he was a fanatic Christian. I noticed he carried a little Bible in his back pocket and little square cards in his front pocket. One day, I got up the nerve to ask about the cards.

"Oh, these are my memory verse cards," he said, clearly pleased I'd asked. "I work on memorizing Bible verses when I'm on watch."

He pulled out his card packet from his pocket and handed it to me.

"Pick a card, tell me the verse, and I'll try to recite it to you."

I pulled a card from the middle of the pack. "Romans 6:23," I said.

Without hesitation, he rattled off, "For the wages of sin is death, but the free gift of God is eternal life in Christ Jesus our Lord."

We smiled at each other.

"God, he is perfect. And so cute!" I thought to myself.

That night, I wrote out my own cards and memorized my first

scripture verse. I couldn't wait to show Jim. He wasn't like other men. He cared about my spirit. He was godly, holy, and joyful, I told myself.

I wanted to learn how to be like him. And to my delight, Jim wanted to teach me. He gave me two little study booklets titled, *Your Life in Christ* and *Walking with Christ*. We'd read a chapter in the Bible, then answer study questions together. He always had an answer to any question I had. He was always at the ready to explain how to live a life that pleased God.

Jim had trained in a Christian organization called The Navigators. Founded by a group of Christian sailors, the organization developed a template for how to disciple (mentor) other Christians. The Navigator Program called for us to do four things:

1. Read, study, and memorize the Bible
2. Pray
3. Attend church faithfully
4. Evangelize—share testimony to save other people.

I focused first on reading my Bible. As a teenager, I was taught to "feel" the Holy Spirit, which was too nebulous for me. Jim taught me a much more structured way to read. He taught me to think of the Bible as God speaking to me when I read it. Then, when I prayed, I was to answer back to God.

"This is how a relationship is grown and developed with God," he explained.

With Jim as my spiritual mentor, I felt reassured that I could connect with God. I felt I could conquer my sins and be a victorious Christian, finally. We spent our free time together, going on walks and talking about the Bible. And we began to fall in love.

He told me his testimony. Of course, it was dramatic. Jesus saved him from addiction and an aching loneliness. When he was saved, he said he'd felt God's love as a warmth flowing over his body. He told me that God's presence had filled the deep loneliness inside him, and he never felt lonely again.

I remember thinking how similar his testimony was to my mom's. "Mom would be very proud of me," I thought. "She'd love Jim."

DEPENDENCY IS A TWO-WAY STREET

Writing this today, I realize that I was so disconnected from myself that even in the most intimate relationship of my life, my main concern was finding a man who would please my mother. It doesn't take a psychologist to see that I was setting up the same relationship—authority-dependent—with Jim that I had with my mom. If I could have objectively observed myself then, the thought "I want to be like him" would have been my first inkling that I was transferring my dependency from Mom to Jim. I didn't just want to know what he knew, I wanted "to be like him." Just as I had always wanted to be like my mom.

Of course, dependency is a two-way street. Jim took pretty easily to the role of authority figure in our relationship. I'm sure he loved having my rapt attention and total agreement. But knowing Jim as I do now, it wasn't for the adulation. It was more because my hanging on his every word reinforced his own faith in his mind. A faith that he, like me, needed in order to survive our past traumas.

As I would learn over time, Jim's upbringing had caused him to develop an avoidant attachment pattern. If you had asked Jim about his parents, however, he would've told you how great they were and how much he admired them (typical for the avoidant pattern). In fact, everybody liked Jim's parents. They were well regarded in the Southern California community where he grew up—coincidentally not too far from mine.

What wasn't visible was that his parents were so busy propping up that happy-family image that, in truth, they were emotionally distant. So while Jim was busy telling himself and everybody else that he was lucky to have such a wonderful family, inside he felt ignored and unloved. As a child, Jim's brain became conflicted and confused by this, so he pushed away the negative feelings and clung to the positive story about his family. That cognitive dissonance resulted in an avoidant attachment style.

Jim became fiercely independent (which is why he was such a hard worker) with an insatiable need for attention that he told himself he didn't want. He had difficulty trusting others enough to bond and form healthy relationships. Thus, that loneliness first drove him to drugs and then to Jesus.

Like me, Jim had taken refuge in the black-and-white, future-focused thinking of our brand of evangelical Christianity. He'd found safe haven there. He found a system in which he not only functioned but flourished. And he, like me, needed to shore up his belief in this system and not have it questioned. He didn't want to look at his past any more than I wanted to look at mine. He wanted to hand his problems to Jesus. We fed off each other's needs, as together we went deeper and deeper into our Christian identity.

As you might imagine, an insecure avoidant attachment (Jim) and an insecure anxious attachment (me) is a common pair. Jim needed to lead; I needed to follow. And neither of us needed a partner who was going to demand emotional intimacy and dredge up past traumas.

MARRIAGE SOLVES EVERYTHING—NOT

We were married in my hometown. My mom and sister took care of everything (no surprise there!). They found the pastor, chose the flowers, got the venue, selected the menu, and decided who the guests would be. They even bought my wedding dress without me. All that was just fine with me.

On the appointed weekend, Jim and I flew in, got married, and then flew off to honeymoon in Hawaii—which Jim had arranged and paid for.

We held hands the whole flight to Hawaii. As far as I was concerned, I was already in paradise, sitting next to my new husband. I didn't know who I was when I married Jim—nor did I care. I'd found a handsome Christian man to take care of me, and I'd made my mom proud. Life couldn't get any better.

Jim and I were happy in our roles as husband and wife. In those first few years, we truly enjoyed each other. We took our marriage relationship very seriously. We both wanted to please God first, and then please each other. I fully transferred my dependence from Mom onto Jim (though my emotional alliance was still with my mom). And I finally felt secure in my salvation. However, I was well aware that security was dependent on my ability to be a good Christian wife.

I had two years left in the navy when we got married. Jim was already out. As a married couple, we instantaneously acquired status within the Christian community. So no matter where we lived, we had a ready-made group of friends. No interpersonal relationship skills required. We would simply join the Bible study group for young married couples, and we were instantly embraced as part of the community.

As we moved around in those early years, in every church we joined, the women were so kind and welcoming. I'd watch and listen as the other women in these groups would share their stories with one another so freely. They'd laugh and bond over their husbands' quirks. They'd also talk seriously and intimately about challenges they faced as Christians, wives, and women. They offered real support to one another.

Older ladies reached out and offered to mentor me—as they understood the early years of marriage can be hard. They offered true friendship. I wanted nothing more than to take it. So I studied the Bible with them, shopped with them, prayed with them. I even called these women my friends. But I never shared one detail about myself or my marriage with any of them. I wanted to. In my head, I went over what I wanted to say, what I wanted to share. I'd even practice it out loud. But once I was face to face with someone, I couldn't do it. So I never did. I never engaged in the kind of honest talk that leads to the close friendships I'd been observing and craving since childhood.

Once again, my trauma kept me hidden behind walls of my own making. The truth was I still felt guilty for the sexual assault in my past and thus deficient as a Christian wife. I froze when I wanted to share. And then I silently wondered to myself for the billionth time, "What was wrong with me?" I relied on Jim's extraversion to make me socially acceptable, just as I had relied on my mom's outgoing personality.

TWO PEAS IN A POD

As with any couple, Jim and I had our problems. Normal marital relationship problems, which meant that we fought over sex and money. Mostly sex.

As husband and wife, we believed we glorified God only when we had sex with each other. But not too far into our marriage, my desire for sex began to wane. It's not that I never wanted it, I just didn't want it as often as Jim did.

Not surprisingly, Jim felt neglected sexually, and that caused our relationship to suffer. I felt angry with him for needing my body, and at the same time, I felt guilty for not providing my body as was my wifely duty. For Jim, sex was how he felt loved and cared for. For me, God only knows what kind of crossed brain circuits were tripped by sex. Neither of us knew how to talk about our feelings—so we didn't. We became resentful instead.

Every time I gave in and had sex with Jim even though I didn't want to, I resented it. Every time Jim wanted to have sex and I rebuffed his advances, he felt rejected. On top of all that was piled a mound of guilt, and we had no idea what to do with it.

Our church and its patriarchal focus made things worse. To this day, I clearly remember a sermon on sex preached by a young, popular pastor whom I admired. With his beautiful wife looking on from the pews, he preached that a man's need for sex was as important to his life as water. He said that men needed to drink water (have sex) regularly and frequently or they would become dehydrated and desiccated. He went on to give this illustration:

> A wife holds a glass of water. When her husband asks for a drink, the wife turns her shoulder and coldly says, "No." The man remains thirsty. His thirst builds because he needs water. He starts to beg, "Please, can I have a drink of water? Please, just a sip?" Finally, the wife rolls her eyes and reluctantly, says, "Oh alright, here." She shoves the glass toward him. The husband feels so grateful and

devours the glass of water. But his wife's initial resistance registers within him. He worries that he might be without a drink for a long time. So, he begins to feel resentment towards his wife.

That was it. Clearly, it was all on the wife to prevent her husband's resentment. If the wife had any resentment or other issues concerning sex or her husband's behavior, the pastor didn't address that.

The memories of that sermon seared permanently into my brain, along with guilt and self-blame. I sat stiffly next to Jim and stared straight ahead after the pastor spoke, because Jim and I both knew that I was the selfish wife refusing Jim his water.

Did we talk about it when we got home? Of course not. Our sexual relationship did not improve one iota. We continued with the status quo—hoping God would heal us. Two peas in a pod.

We didn't see it then. But our sexual relationship re-enacted our childhood traumas. Jim felt rejected (his childhood wound). And I felt like a failure, wanting but unable to please the person I was dependent on (my childhood wound).

No God or religion could fix that. That would be up to us, as individuals. But neither Jim nor I wanted to hear or accept that truth—and we trusted each other not to bring it up.

When you cling to an outside belief, institution, or set of rules for your emotional security, you naturally are attracted to others who are doing the same and so won't challenge you. The problem is that living in that kind of denial together only serves to compound your traumas, not heal them.

It was like Jim and I lived on a leaking boat, and we kept fixing the sails. What we needed to do was learn how to scuba dive, so we could get underneath the boat to fix the true cause of our pain. Eventually, psychotherapy supplied our scuba lessons, but that wouldn't come for either of us for decades.

Despite our issues, Jim and I loved each other and were committed to our marriage. You could argue that our aversion to conflict worked for us in those early years, keeping us from hurting each other too much. But it also kept us from really knowing each other and knowing ourselves—and it kept our traumas very much alive, a malevolent force in the dynamic of our marriage.

As long as it was just the two of us, however, we could keep up the façade. After all, our lives were so nicely structured, with God being the answer for everything. There was no one to challenge us when we hid behind church doctrine. We certainly weren't going to call each other out to face reality. There were no issues in our lives that couldn't be swept under the righteous rug Jesus laid out for us.

Then came children.

EXERCISE

How Your Dominant Attachment Pattern Affects Your Relationships

Your attachment style—secure, avoidant, anxious, or disorganized, all of which we discussed at length in Chapter 5—reveals itself in your adult relationship through your reactions to conflict, arguments, and disagreements.

Securely attached people argue the facts and work toward resolution. Their egos aren't involved, and they don't need to be right, only to come to an understanding of what's right. Not too many of us fall into that category. Most of us are either avoidant, like Jim, or anxious, like me. (People with disorganized attachment have a host of reactions to conflict too diverse and complicated to explore in this exercise.)

As we heal our trauma and move toward a more secure pattern, how we approach conflict improves as well. To help you see what this growth might look like in yourself, Jim and I have written out what we used to think when we fought early in our relationship, and what our internal conversation is now when we have conflict.

Remember, attachment patterns are not black-and-white. But during stress, your tendency will be to revert back to your default childhood responses.

How anxiously attached Dorothy argued with Jim in the past:
- When Jim and I get into an argument or disagreement, I tend to worry, think about, and try to figure out how he feels about me and what I can do to make him feel better.
- When I have a problem, I reach out to Jim immediately.
- I think about Jim throughout the day. I think about what he's doing and if he's okay.
- I will defer to Jim's desires, hobbies, and entertainment choices because that's what makes me happy.
- If Jim becomes unhappy, I worry about my security.

How avoidantly attached Jim argued with Dorothy in the past:
- When Dorothy and I get into an argument or disagreement, I try to avoid it with humor or by being too busy with work.
- When I have a problem, I try to fix it myself. Asking for help is like the proverbial asking for directions—I'll drive and drive before I ask for help.
- I don't think much about Dorothy throughout the day.
- I find myself always taking charge of decisions, which makes me a little resentful.
- If Dorothy becomes unhappy, I feel really, really uncomfortable, which leads me to withdraw and I avoid addressing it.

How more secure Dorothy and Jim argue today:
Dorothy – Today, when we get into an argument or disagreement, I listen to what Jim is saying and feeling. I sometimes ask

a question or two so that I can understand his point of view. I try to figure out why I'm angry or scared or feel hurt. Then, I try to explain my point of view to Jim. I look for a solution that's best for me. I don't worry about Jim or think about him very much during the day. I feel assured he's okay and can handle the problems he encounters. I no longer feel responsible for him.

Jim – Today, when we get into an argument or disagreement, I'm better able to remain present and validate Dorothy's feelings. I also try to be more open about my own needs and risk rejection by expressing them. Even though Dorothy may not agree with me or meet my needs the way I want, at least we understand each other. I do think about her during the day and reach out from time to time. I get frustrated, though, because she generally doesn't answer calls and doesn't check her texts as often as I'd like. Overall, the increased openness to express my needs and feelings creates more relational security, which lessens my fear.

How do you argue?

Think about the last argument you had:
- What thoughts did you have that perhaps were expressions of avoidant attachment or anxious attachment?
- What thoughts allowed you to be a victim or made you feel righteous?
- What arguments did you make that weren't productive in furthering understanding?

Write them down and study them. These thoughts most likely come from your attachment pattern and get in the way of problem-solving.

Chapter 8

TRAUMA: THE NEXT GENERATION

After my stint in the navy was up, Jim decided we should become missionaries. He didn't decide this by himself. His mentor—which all members of the Navigators have—suggested it. Our training would take place at the Navigators Leadership Development Institute's (LDI) headquarters in Colorado Springs. We'd be given room, board, and training. To cover all other expenses, we were to solicit friends and family for a monthly stipend.

Though I never would have expressed it and barely allowed myself to think it, I didn't want to go. I didn't believe I had what it took to lead someone else to Jesus. I was still being led by Jim. But I did believe that it was my duty as a Christian wife to support my husband in whatever career path he chose. So off we went.

I have to admit that the time we spent at LDI was magical. We lived on the grounds of the headquarters, the beautiful Glen Eyrie Castle. We woke every morning to a view of endless rolling green lawns with the occasional herd of big horn sheep nestled in the tall mountain cliffs. To get to class, we strolled along circular paths that connected a series of old cobblestone buildings. As married students, we, of course, had special status. Our social activities, Bible study group, and support group were separate from those attended by single students. We had our own teachers and mentors too. A ready-made community.

Life was pretty ideal for two broke kids just out of the navy. Or so it looked from the outside. As time went on, I was feeling more and more insecure about money. I knew our financial instability made my mother unhappy. So it became something I worried about. At the same time, I convinced myself this was a test of faith. If I were doing as God commanded, I'd have full faith in God's ability to provide. Which, as our brand of Christianity always did, put the focus, the responsibility, and the blame for our lack of resources back on me and my incompetence in being a good Christian. Needless to say, I wasn't finding the comfort I'd once found in Jesus. I was finding a lot of judgment that fed my trauma brain—judgment I believed I deserved.

Near the end of our training, Jim informed me he didn't want to be a missionary. Whew. He wanted to be a preacher. That sounded okay. So he'd need to go to college. That sounded expensive. And not conducive to saving money or starting a family, which is what I felt the need to do.

He talked with his mentor, and they decided Jim would attend Covenant College, a small, Christian liberal arts school in Chattanooga, Tennessee. I talked with my mentor, and we decided I would be supportive of whatever Jim wanted to do. So that was that.

A month before we left LDI, to our delight, our daughter Emma was born. Her brother, Dustin, would come along three years later, in Jim's senior year at Covenant.

MY TRAUMA DOESN'T DO PROBLEMS

As with everything else in my life, I didn't put a lot of thought into parenting. I looked to my Christian community for direction. I joined the "young moms" group at our church. I also depended on Jim, a lot.

I loved and enjoyed our children. I'd even say I was a good mom, as long as there were no complications. But when the slightest problem arose—such as one of them having a meltdown in the grocery aisle or the daycare calling because one or both had a fever—I went right into

FFFF. I'd freeze and do nothing. Try as I might, I couldn't overcome this automatic reaction...or stop judging myself for having it.

When our kids cried out or got sick in the middle of the night, Jim went to them, not me. I didn't open an eye. He'd tell me about it the next day, always to my surprise. He never woke me up. And I never insisted on his doing so. Somehow, we both knew instinctively that when it came to the children, it was best if he took care of problems on his own.

I knew from listening to other moms at Bible study that this arrangement with Jim was unusual. When the other moms shared their kid stories, mom always knew what to do and dad was clueless. I never shared with the group or anyone that I was the "clueless" parent in our family. I simply added it to my shame pile and gave my trauma another secret to feed on.

GONE MOM

Jim graduated from Covenant with a degree in history and the notion that now God was calling him to be a college professor. Which would mean earning a PhD. Which would mean we were looking at four more years of poverty. So when he didn't get into the specific program that he felt God had called him to, I was secretly relieved.

While Jim was deciding what was next for us, we moved our little family back to California. There I'd have the support of my mother, which I was desperate for.

We stayed with my parents for a few months in Orange County. Once we both landed steady work—Jim full-time, me part-time—we moved into a double-wide in the less expensive community of Corona.

Before I could breathe a sigh of relief that we were finally settled, Jim decided to add law school to his already full schedule. I smiled (as trauma had conditioned me to do) when he announced this, but my anxiety went through the roof. Not about finances this time—I knew we could swing the expense, and investing in Jim was always a smart move. But because this meant that, in addition to being gone all day every day at work, he'd be in class three nights a week. I'd be taking on more responsibility for the children. What if something happened and Jim was in class?

Make no mistake: I was the problem here. Emma and Dustin were good kids. But my trauma kept insidiously telling me how incompetent I was. And I was a good enough mother not to want my children's caregiver (me) to be incompetent. The simplest of things—like being in charge of the snack at Emma's daycare—set off alarm bells. What would be appropriate? Should I make it or buy it? What if the children hate it and then hate Emma? What will the other parents think? On and on my mind would spin. My PTSD would then toss foreboding into the mix—all leading me back to my constant companion, the perennial question, "What's wrong with me?"

During those years, I did everything I could to put my children's care in someone else's hands. I scheduled playdates. I'd leave them with my parents as often as they'd let me. If there was a vacation Bible school, Sunday school, or an afterschool program at church, I'd sign them up.

Jim hired teenagers from our neighborhood to watch the children between the time I left for work in the afternoons and when he got home—which on his school nights might not be until after ten. I never felt comfortable about this arrangement. Dustin, who was three, was too small to be looked after by a teenager at night. But I never said anything because I didn't have another solution.

One night I got a call at my work from the babysitter's mother. Dustin had hit his head and needed stitches. They were at the hospital. She explained she'd tried to get ahold of Jim, but he wasn't answering his pager. Once I'd made sure Dustin was okay, I thanked her for taking him to get stitches and that was that. I didn't leave work. I didn't rush to the hospital. I had more faith in a neighbor I barely knew than myself to handle this crisis. I didn't attune to Dustin's need, which was probably for his mother. (And by the way, this isn't all on me. What kind of parent turns off his pager knowing he has two small children at home with a teenage babysitter? Answer: One with an avoidant attachment pattern.)

Emma and Dustin, as children do, felt my anxiety. Worse, anytime I was challenged, they'd watch me freeze. A glazed look in my eye. A smile on my face. And no action to resolve whatever put me in that state. To them, Mom was "gone" again.

When unhealed trauma hijacks our thinking, we're prevented from seeing the reality of a situation, weighing our options rationally, and taking effective action. When our trauma story injects its old fear into the present moment, it defines our goals for that moment, which directs our actions and limits our lives: Keep me safe (when we are perfectly safe). Don't let me stand out (when no one is looking at us—and so what if they are?). I couldn't possibly do that (when we're perfectly capable). And the mother of them all: If anyone really knew me, they'd reject me (when the truth is, it's the behaviors our hijacked brains automatically select for us that keep us from meaningful relationships).

Once I was in that state in front of my children, I wasn't attending to the issue at hand. I wasn't able to model good life management for them, let alone guide them in understanding their challenges. I was so in my own head that I couldn't attune to their perspective. I couldn't meet their emotional needs. I couldn't give them the words they needed to organize and express their feelings. I was inept at comforting and protecting them. I also had trouble playing with them or simply being with them. When I froze, all I could do was drag Emma and Dustin into my trauma with me—just as my traumatized mother had dragged me into hers.

When trauma drives our thinking and behavior, no one, including ourselves, can really know us. Thus, no one, including our children, can securely attach to us, guaranteeing the intergenerational transfer of trauma.

UPSIDE-DOWN PARENTING

Since I was incapable of calming myself down, Emma and Dustin had to adjust to my nervous system. Since I was unavailable to help them with their emotional needs, they had to adjust to my emotional needs. Their brains had to find their own way back to calm.

Emma, who was seemingly born capable, did this by assuming the role of parent. It was she, not me, who kept tabs on the details of our day: "Mom, don't forget the tickets." "Mom, Bible camp starts next Monday." "Mom, we need milk."

On her first day of kindergarten, Emma stood in our kitchen looking picture perfect in her school uniform. My beautiful five-year-old had dressed herself. I can remember thinking how grateful I was that they had to wear uniforms: Fewer decisions for me!

I packed Dustin in the car first, along with his stroller. I leafed through the paperwork for the fifth time, making sure all the papers were there. I accounted for all the appropriate signatures and left no question unanswered. I was the one who was nervous.

Emma was full of questions as we drove to school. I tried to answer. But the truth was I did not have the answers, which added to my anxiety. I hoped the other mothers would be in the same boat.

When we arrived, the line of moms and kids waiting to register was so long that I couldn't see the front of it. I wasn't sure this was where we were supposed to be, but I was too self-conscious to ask anyone. So I took my place in the back of the line with Emma beside me and Dustin in his stroller.

After about fifteen minutes, Emma slipped her hand out of mine and took off. It looked like she was headed toward the front. I called after her. But she kept going. She didn't look back or acknowledge me. Eventually, neither I nor the other moms standing near me could see her anymore.

People started looking at me. My trauma brain felt threatened by their stares. "Don't stand out, don't stand out," it kept repeating. In reality their looks were probably more out of boredom, curiosity, or concern than threat. But my mind raced. My blood pressure spiked. My rapid body memory took over. I froze. I was "gone."

As I stood motionless with a smile on my face, internally, I was freaking out. "What should I do? Why did she leave me?" My mind raced through different solutions. I could call out for her. I could leave the line and go check on her. But I was unable to act.

Jumping out of line would only bring more attention to me. My trauma brain couldn't tolerate that because, in my mind, being noticed was akin to a life-threatening situation. (Something had caused my assailant to choose me over the other children all those years ago. My brain wasn't going to allow me to stand out again.) Though I couldn't bear the thought of looking so incompetent in front of the other parents, I stayed put. I told myself that Emma would come back in a minute. But she didn't.

After several more minutes, I began drawing more attention by not moving. So my trauma brain made the decision to go look for Emma. I found her at the check-in table, looking at her teacher. Her teacher asked if I was Emma's mother. I said, "yes," and she checked Emma in. No big deal. Still, I was embarrassed and upset. I cloaked the reason for my distress in manners—Emma cut in line and that was rude. But what was really upsetting my brain was that Emma's actions had drawn attention to us and that was dangerous.

As I look at this event now through the lens of attachment, I can see that Emma felt my anxiety about not knowing if we were in the right line, which made *her* anxious. So, she took charge. She flip-flopped our roles. She became the parent. In psychological terms, this is known as upside-down parenting.

Afterward, I tried to forget the incident. I didn't talk to Emma about it. I never asked her why she felt the need to go to the front of the line or if she was scared when she couldn't see me. I never told her that it scared me when I couldn't see her. I certainly never asked myself why I let my five-year-old out of my sight in a strange environment. My trauma kept me silent; that's what trauma does.

This is how seemingly benign events work to transfer intergenerational insecurity and trauma from parent to child. Though Emma acted like a "super child," you can bet she felt just as scared as I did that day. She was only five years old and desperately needed her mom to take care of her. But I was "gone." So she took care of me.

Emma would find it necessary to perform upside-down parenting a thousand times throughout her childhood. The attachment style Emma developed was avoidant, just like Jim's.

WHEN TRAUMA DOES THE PARENTING

Dustin adapted differently. He was and still is more sensitive in the world—an observer, and a deep thinker. He identified with my anxiety more and would withdraw when I became upset or "gone."

One such occasion stands out in my mind because I feel guilty about it to this day. Dustin, Emma, and I were invited to an amusement park to celebrate Emma's best friend's birthday. As soon as we arrived, Emma ran off to be with her friends. Being only five, Dustin stayed with me. As we approached the group of moms and toddlers, he got so excited about the park and its exhibits that his voice went up an octave or two as he expressed his delight to me. Instead of sharing in his excitement and laughing about the high-pitched tone of his voice, I got embarrassed and inexplicably triggered.

At first, I asked him quietly, "Why are you talking like a baby?" Too enthralled with his surroundings, he didn't hear me and kept talking in this squeaky voice. So I bent down, held his hand roughly, and hissed in anger, "Stop talking like a baby!"

He didn't really understand what I was asking or why. But he did comprehend that I was upset. So to calm me and bring safety to all, he shut down. All his beautiful little boy enthusiasm and joy completely left his body. He slumped his shoulders, lowered his head, and never said another word at the party.

Of course, I was smiling by this point and trying to pretend nothing happened. For the rest of the party, I continued on as if we were just fine and having a good time. Dustin did not bounce back to his normal self.

As we drove home, I began to feel remorse. Dustin didn't deserve what I'd done to him. I realized I'd made a mistake correcting him. Yet, I didn't apologize or try to repair the damage done.

To this day, I don't understand what about his voice that day triggered me into shame. I do know it was a trigger, because my reaction was completely over the top and unattuned to what was taking place from Dustin's perspective. I treated Dustin too harshly because I was self-conscious. My need to project some image overrode my son's happiness—and my ability to share in that happiness. I pushed and pulled on him until he complied and joined me in FFFF.

You'd be right to say that's hardly child abuse. I made a mistake; all parents do. But here's the thing: Traumatized parents make more mistakes and, more importantly, traumatized parents don't know how to repair their mistakes.

The emotional wounds I caused that day in Dustin remained opened, helping him to form false beliefs about himself as he grew: "I shouldn't feel happy." "Don't draw attention to myself." "There's something wrong with me." "It's not safe for me to share my feelings."

Securely attached parents, when they recognize their mistakes, move quickly toward their children, revisit what happened, apologize, and allow their children to process their feelings. If I had apologized to Dustin that day, he'd have learned that his feelings were valid and important. He'd have understood the true cause of his hurt feelings was that Mom made a mistake. And lastly, he'd have learned—because I would have been modeling—how to repair and rebound from his own mistakes.

But I didn't do any of that. I did what I saw my parents do, what my church encouraged me to do. I apologized to God. I asked Jesus to forgive me of my sins (mistakes). This did nothing to heal Dustin or help him to develop a positive sense of self. What it did do was allow my trauma and insecurities to pass unimpeded to my son—and they did. Dustin became anxiously attached, like me.

BORN BAD

As a Christian parent, I was told my children were born sinners thanks to original sin. Thus, my primary job as their mother was to save my children from hell. I was to teach them to repent and accept Jesus as their savior. It was up to me to bring them up in the ways of the Lord, so as they grew, they would not depart from His way.

Not feeling secure in my ability to do that, I absorbed the parenting teachings of evangelical preachers such as Pat Robertson, Jerry Falwell, and Dr. James Dobson. Dobson's organization, Focus on the Family, put out books with titles such as *Dare to Discipline* and *The Strong-Willed Child*. The titles supported the Christian theory that original sin motivates children to be bad and rebel against God. I was to enact strong discipline in the home (as opposed to loving guidance) and enforce good behavior (as opposed to helping them cultivate self-discipline).

To no one's surprise, I wasn't very good at "enforcing" anything. Luckily, with Emma and Dustin, I didn't really need to. If either was motivated to be "bad and rebel against God," I never experienced it when they were small. They lived—as most kids do—to please Jim and me. They happily participated in church, and they dutifully followed the rules.

As our children grew, Jim and I wanted nothing more than to impart our Christian identity onto them. Like all parents, we wanted to keep them from harm and ensure their happiness. To us, Christianity guaranteed that. After all, our Christian identity had lifted both of us out of very dark places, given us the supportive community we needed to function, and put us on a path to a righteous life—a life of structure and safety.

AND THE LITTLE CHILD SHALL LEAD THEM

My first inkling that my children might not find that same strength in our religion came when Emma was about fourteen. Developmentally right on target, she was spreading her wings, meeting new people, wanting to do things outside the church and our family, and searching for an identity of her own. Because I didn't understand this and because my trauma brain kicked in when she requested to do anything outside my comfort zone, instead of guiding her into adulthood, my reactions served to confuse her process.

A few years ago, adult Emma informed me that her breaking point came when she and I were fighting about her going to a three-day concert in another town with her friend and no parents.

"Mom, pleeease! Just talk to my friend's mom," teenage Emma had been pleading for days.

"Okay, I'll do that. But I don't think that will change my mind," I said over and over again.

For anyone who has had a teenager or remembers their own teenage years, there's nothing unusual about this argument. As her mother, I had every reason to deny her permission. But Emma needed more than that; she needed to know why. With no understanding between us, the argument escalated. And of course with all the tension, I froze. Gone.

Incensed and probably fed up with my inability to be present when she needed me, she got in my face and shouted, "Do something!"

Her face was red and streaked with tears. My face was still and blank.

Emma ran outside. Jim ran after her. I stood there scared and motionless. I could hear them yelling and running around the house. I hid in the little laundry room like a frightened child. I heard some neighbors get involved. Then the police came. Then the police left. The neighbors went home. And poor Emma was left crying by herself. I felt helpless. I blamed myself. I feared that I'd created the same chaotic family situation I'd been raised in.

Unbeknownst to Emma, at this point, she wasn't fighting me, she was fighting my trauma. Her going away without me to a place where there'd probably be boys triggered memories of my mother packing me off to Europe. I was scared that Emma could be harmed the same way I'd been. But I didn't explain that to her. I just said "no," and left her to figure it out for herself.

So her teenage brain figured that if all her years of being a good girl had not earned our trust, what's the point of being good?

And why shouldn't she think that. That's how we'd raised her. Our Christian authoritarian parenting model had given her that reward and punishment mindset. To her way of thinking, getting to go to this concert was akin to an earned right. So why follow any rules if there's no reward?

An attuned me could've explained that it wasn't that I didn't trust her, it was that I didn't trust other people who might be at the concert. They might present dangerous situations, adult situations that she and her friend were too young to manage on their own. Emma might still have been angry with me, but at least she'd see there was solid reasoning behind my decision. Unfortunately, my trauma brain (as with all traumatized brains) couldn't access reasoning to make a coherent decision.

Instead of seeing her as the individual she was becoming and responding to her in a way that would help her mature, I doubled down on my Christian parenting skills and insisted on more church, more prayer, and more Bible. I had no idea this emerging self of hers—which often showed up as defiance—was normal for an adolescent. All I could see in her behavior was rebellion against God. And that scared me for her.

As I clung to our religion as the answer to all things, my relationship with Emma rotted away. Emma became distant, burying her anger. She became closed off to us, unwilling to trust us any longer. She sought belonging outside our home and outside the church. The natural progression of our insecure relationship had brought us to this point: conflict without resolution, without solution, without compromise, without discussion. And then I swept it all under the rug, ensuring we didn't repair the rupture in our relationship.

Emma started sneaking out at night. She got bad grades for the first time in her life. She was smoking and drinking. She took the car without our permission. And she skipped school so much that I, an attorney's wife, was threatened with arrest for her truancy.

Jim and I were beside ourselves. Not knowing what to do, we did what we always did—we kept looking to our church for answers and direction. But our pastor, church counselors, and fellow parishioners said the same things over and over again: "You're good parents." "Just keep praying." "Give it over to Jesus." We were told to be strong with her and hold to our boundaries. While that may work with a ten-year-old, how was I supposed to physically restrain a teenager?

Our daughter was in danger and their words were useless. Our brand of Christianity was failing us. More importantly, it was failing Emma.

Our religion asked us to believe that only Jesus—an outside force—could heal us. For years, both Jim and I had believed that wholeheartedly, even when God's love made us feel pretty bad about ourselves. Ironically, it took another force, an inside force—our love for Emma—to show us the limitations of that thinking. Though we were far from knowing it at that moment, Jim and I would both have to turn inward and find the answers within ourselves if we were to help Emma (and eventually ourselves). That would mean departing from God—at least our church's version of Him—and bringing ourselves up in the ways of self-love, self-realization, and self-acceptance.

Today, I regard our church's version of Christianity as a stepping-stone to my recovery from trauma. At a very stress-filled and chaotic time in my life, our church gave me a structure that allowed me to function. Our Christian philosophy of life and relationships dovetailed perfectly with my trauma's search for certainty and security. Have faith in Jesus (rely on others). Follow Jesus (obey God's commandments). And become an active member of the church (remain hidden in the middle of the herd).

However, I was outgrowing that structure—with my children leading the way. Three years behind Emma, Dustin too would pull away from our church, although he was much quieter about it.

EXERCISE

The Kid-Parent Relationship

Having a clear picture of what we thought of our parents when we were children puts us in touch with our inner-child's life and helps us to heal our trauma today. So get out a pen and paper, and take these four steps to help you get clearer on your childhood:

- *Step one:* Write down five words that describe your childhood relationship with your mom.
- *Step two:* Choose two of the words and write about a specific memory that illustrates each.
- *Step three:* Write down five words that describe your childhood relationship with your dad.
- *Step four:* Choose two words and write about a specific memory that illustrates each.

As you read over what you've written, what do you see about your relationship with your parents now that you may not have noticed before? How does that inform you?

Chapter 9

RE-PARENTING MYSELF

As our children were coming into their own, Jim started the two of us down a path of realization and transformation as well—though neither of us knew it at the time.

After a twentieth wedding anniversary cruise to Alaska, Jim mentioned that he wanted us to become psychotherapists. On the cruise, we'd spent quite a bit of time with this wonderful older couple. Both of them were marriage and family therapists. They told us their work was not only endlessly interesting, but also allowed them to arrange their schedule so they could travel. I thought Jim was just musing about a way to have more flexibility and less responsibility in his life. I giggled and ignored his comment.

Over the course of several months, however, he kept bringing it up—adding that if we both became therapists, our combined income would be sufficient to maintain our standard of living. I kept giggling and ignoring. But as the idea pushed its way into our conversations more and more frequently, I started to worry. We were doing really well. Jim's law practice was booming. I worked for him (meaning I didn't have to go out in the world and get a job). We had a good-sized nest egg. The children were almost grown. If he went back to school and changed careers, it might be like starting over again. Also, I'd be a full and equal partner in our family's finances. Not to mention, I didn't believe I had it in me to help people with real problems. All this sounded like a lot of responsibility.

Eventually, Jim stopped floating the idea and tied it down for me. He told me he was exhausted and stressed. If he kept practicing law, he feared he'd have a heart attack within ten years. He'd always had an interest in psychology—almost majoring in it instead of history (something I hadn't known). He sincerely wanted to see if it could be a career path for us both.

Inside, I was panicking a little. I didn't want to lose my standing as the wife of a successful attorney. I certainly didn't want to have to find a job. I didn't want to be poor again. But I didn't want him to have a heart attack either. In addition to loving Jim, I was completely dependent on him. He was the one who made friends easily. He was the one everyone at church respected. He was the one who made money. I could not and did not want to live without him. So I agreed we'd go to school. I'd deal with actually practicing psychotherapy when we got there—if I ever got there.

REALIZATION

Jim had already found a program for us at California Baptist University. Though psychotherapy wasn't something our sect of Christianity approved of, other sects were opening up to it as long as the counseling was based in biblical principles, which Cal Baptist's program was.

Jim and I attended all our classes together. We learned about family systems, child therapy, and pathologies. We studied the DSM-5 and learned to diagnose mental disorders. We talked about ethics and the law regarding marriage and family therapists. We learned to give our clients "unconditional positive regard"—meaning we would never look shocked by or disdainful of anything anyone said, no matter what we thought. Bottom line: We learned basic talk therapy—which meant that clients would look to me as a resource, the one who's supposed to know how to heal them.

That scared me. How could I, with all my anxiety and self-doubt, be a resource for better mental health for anyone? I can remember many professors saying, "You're already a counselor. You've entered into this program because friends and family naturally come to you for advice." That was probably true for most of my classmates—it was certainly true of Jim—but no one had ever come to me looking for advice. If they had, I wouldn't have known what to say.

At the start of the program, part of our coursework was to experience therapy as a patient. That's when I found Anne, who invited me to consider I might have PTSD. In our last few years of school, we were required to do a 600-hour practicum under a licensed therapist and treat clients ourselves under supervision. Yikes.

To help us find a supervisor, the school had a big fair with all the local mental health agencies, all the churches with Christian counseling programs, and people from the university's mental health clinic. As we talked to the different groups, Jim and I agreed we wanted to train together. We wanted it to be Christian—so we only applied to the church programs and Cal Baptist's clinic. We got an interview with every practice we applied to. But to our great shock, we got no offers.

AVIS AND THE BRAVE NEW WORLD

Jim and I didn't have a Plan B. If we were going to graduate on time, we needed to find a supervisor—and soon. One afternoon, as I stood in line at Starbucks, I overheard the woman behind me talking about supervision, of all things! I inconspicuously looked over my shoulder. She was from our class. I knew her.

"Oh, hi," I said, which was extremely out of character for me, but that's how desperate I felt.

When my classmate introduced me to the licensed therapist she was asking to supervise her, I blurted out, "My husband and I are looking for a supervisor, too. Can we apply to your program?"

"Absolutely," she said and gave me her card.

That's how I met Avis.

Over the next few weeks, Avis accepted a small group of trainees into her growing marriage and family therapy practice—including Jim and me. A natural born teacher, she taught us the hard skills and soft skills of conducting effective therapy. She taught us everything from filling out the proper paperwork, to how to calm clients who are meeting us for the first time, to how to form trust in the client-therapist relationship.

Avis wasn't about systems, strict protocols, and dependence on the talk therapy we were learning in school. She wanted us to find the therapy or approach that worked best for each client. She exposed us to attachment-based parenting and positive discipline—both revolutionary concepts to a Christian like me. She kept abreast of the latest studies, theories, and therapies, and made sure we were up-to-date, too.

Though Avis had taken me step-by-step through her process, when it came time for me to see clients by myself, I was terrified. The thought of someone looking to me for help sent me into FFFF. Avis saw my apprehension. So when I asked her if I could see clients with Jim, she agreed. We'd counsel couples as a couple. While this might seem like enabling my trauma, what she was really doing is a therapeutic technique called "scaffolding"—giving me the extra support I needed until I could counsel on my own.

Jim and I graduated in 2012, and Avis became our mentor, overseeing our three years of required internship.

Also perfect and rather serendipitous for me was that Avis's specialty was trauma therapy. She had an insatiable thirst for new research in the field. And Jim and I were right there with her. If she recommended a lecture, we went to it. If she thought a workshop looked interesting, we took it.

In particular, she was interested in mind-body therapies, which use the body as an avenue to reach those hidden places in our minds and produce healing faster. She introduced Jim and me to emotional freedom therapy (EFT)—commonly known as "tapping"—a body-centered way to disrupt a stuck mental pattern. She was also getting great results with eye movement desensitization and reprocessing therapy (EMDR).

EMDR takes advantage of the fact that our eyes move in a certain pattern when our brains are triggered. The client follows the therapist's hand as it moves back and forth in front of the client's eyes. Once in the pattern, the client is able to access their trauma and release their fear without going into FFFF. Researchers don't really know what the back-and-forth movement does, but they know it works. EMDR was developed as a therapy for PTSD, and over the years it has proven efficient and effective for a variety of conditions.

Avis invited us—along with a few other interns in our area—to attend a five-day training in Tucson, an offshoot of EMDR called brainspotting. We both wanted to go but Jim ended up having a conflict. Though I was afraid to travel without him, I really wanted to learn this. So I gathered up my courage and went.

MAKING THE MIND-BODY CONNECTION

I had packed a cooler full of sandwiches, so I wouldn't have to eat lunch with anyone I didn't know. I had brought my Bible and my Christian tapes to give me structure and support during my time away. (I had promised myself to carve out quiet time for God every day.) Still, with no Jim to hide behind, I knew I'd end up having to talk to my traveling companions.

This turned out to not be as painful as I'd imagined. They were all therapists in training, so they were pretty easy to talk to. I especially liked a woman named Tillie, and I got to know Avis as a person, not just as a mentor.

The training in Tucson consisted of mornings filled with lectures on brainspotting techniques. Afternoons were dedicated to practicing what we'd learned on each other.

That first morning, our instructor explained that brainspotting was originally developed by David Grand for treating childhood trauma. Like EMDR, it uses eye patterns—Grand uses an actual pointer and has clients follow it with their eyes to tap into their midbrain. Unlike EMDR, however, brainspotting has the client use one fixed eye position. Clients often twitch when they hit that trauma position. Then, the therapist has them keep their eyes there and let the position do the work.

Our instructor taught a version of brainspotting she called resourcing brainspotting. She didn't use a pointer or the clients' eyes. She used music going from ear to ear—known as bilateral music. She stressed that the client's body is the resource here, and we as therapists are teaching our clients to activate that resource and heal themselves.

During her presentation, she called on a person from the audience, a woman in her sixties. Our instructor asked the woman what she felt in her body. As she guided the woman through the therapeutic protocol, that feeling ended up correlating to a childhood event in the woman's life. As we watched, the woman seemed to physically become a small child. She curled up in her seat. By asking more questions, the therapist helped the woman to remain in that state. The woman talked like a little girl as she explored an emotionally scarring event from her childhood. When the session was over, the woman claimed she felt relief.

I was skeptical. That seemed a little too fast for a breakthrough, let alone a healing. Also, to the Christian in me, this was all a little too new agey. So after our debriefing, I got up the nerve and asked our instructor and the volunteer whether they knew each other, and had been working together awhile. They both responded no, they'd never met before today, that this had been a one-time event. Further, our instructor said the volunteer's results were not uncommon at all. Still, I remained skeptical.

THE RE-PARENTING

That afternoon, we attendees took a crack at brainspotting. Tillie and I decided to partner—with me as the client first and she as the therapist. We turned our chairs so we'd be face to face, our knees inches part. I put some earphones in, allowing bilateral music to move gently back and forth from my right ear to my left. I closed my eyes and started to tune into the rhythm of my breath—slow, deep, and steady. I could hear our instructor moving about the room offering suggestions and advice to the other dyads of training therapists.

"What are you feeling in your body?" Tillie asked.

I took a moment to check. "I feel tightness in my stomach."

She guided me to breathe into my stomach and asked, "What age does this tightness feel?"

An image of myself at six years old immediately formed in my head. "I feel six."

I sensed Tillie looking at her instruction book so she could guide me along the treatment protocol.

"Okay," she continued. "Look into your six-year-old's eyes and breathe together."

As I followed her instructions, I felt the emotions of my six-year-old self—her fear, her sadness, her confusion. And then something I had not felt before—like I wasn't alone. I felt the fear of dying alone lift off of my body. I suddenly knew that if I had died that day of the assault, I wouldn't have died alone. And then Jesus appeared. My adult-self observed my six-year-old self with Jesus. In my mind, I stood opposite Jesus as He held my six-year-old's hand. Adult me in real life began crying.

In my mind I asked Jesus, "Were you really there?"

Jesus looked at me and replied, "Yes, I was there with you. You would not have died alone. I was there with you. You were not alone."

I felt wonderfully relieved and reassured by the presence and connection with another being.

I continued to cry. I had never cried before about what happened to me. I rarely cried at all, only when watching movies or reading books. My tears flowed freely now. It felt good. The fear of dying alone had been a major source of my trauma, always with me, right behind my eyes, in the shadows of my mind. And with that one session, delivered by a fellow trainee, I'd released that old fear and changed the emotional memory of what happened to me so long ago.

"What do you feel in your stomach now?" Tillie asked.

I moved my attention to my physical body and breathed into my stomach. I felt cared for and without shame.

"My stomach feels relaxed and warm. The tightness is gone."

"Take a deep breath," Tillie said, continuing to read from the instructions. "And ask your body, 'What is my new truth?'"

I had no doubt about the answer: "I am not alone."

With those four little words, I gave six-year-old me what she'd needed from her mother all those years ago. In other words, I was using this brainspotting therapy to "re-parent" myself successfully through a childhood trauma, transforming my anxious attachment pattern into a more secure pattern. Though I could not yet get my head around what was happening to me, I could feel in my body that my healing from trauma had begun in earnest.

RE-PARENTING: DAY TWO AND THREE

Day two, Tillie and I set an intention to work on a certain issue in the afternoon session. I wanted to work on my "mother wounds." But when we sat down knee to knee, it was my dad, who had died several years earlier, who presented himself in my mind. Clearly, my body had decided that my mother wounds were a little too deep to take on at this stage of my healing journey.

"I love you," my dad said. Then, he apologized for not being able to say those words to me while he was alive. He told me he was with Jesus in heaven. We cried together. My tears connected me to my feelings.

Hearing those words from my dad gave me new understanding and compassion for him. I could feel that that bridge of connection he'd been missing between himself and other people had now formed and healed him. He was finally able to attach.

I found closure around my feelings for him.

Day three, we were instructed to connect with our younger self—to look into our younger self's eyes, breathe together, feel our hearts beating together, and hold each other.

Though I had no idea where this session would lead, I once again chose the six-year-old me. When I looked into my child-self's eyes, I fully felt her feelings...a deep loneliness, longing, and shame all mixed together. And once again, I began to cry.

Tillie instructed my adult self to comfort my child self. When I did, something shifted. I released all the negative feelings about myself that I'd repressed and denied for so long. I felt relieved and validated. I realized for the first time ever that my life mattered. That I mattered. That all my pain, my experiences, all of me mattered.

The knot in my stomach that I'd carried around for more than four decades relaxed. What I was feeling in my body was unconditional love and unconditional acceptance for myself. And it felt far more sacred and better than anything I'd experienced in church. I felt fantastic and was soaking it all in like a parched sponge.

If you would have questioned me about the origins of higher love at that time, I'd have told you it wasn't possible to give ourselves that kind of love. I would have said, as I had learned and believed, that such a love could only come from God.

But that's the thing about the healing produced by mind-body therapies: You don't have to intellectually get it. It doesn't have to jibe with your worldview or your religious beliefs. You don't have to make sense of it, because you can feel its truth. It would literally take me years to understand and integrate what happened for me in those few sessions, but the rewards were immediate.

THE REFINING

On day four, Tillie and I decided we'd try working with other partners. This session produced no miracles for me, but I did learn what *not* to do.

The task at hand was to connect with ourselves during a troubled time. I chose my ten-year-old self. I was chubby back then, and ten was about the age I boarded the diet rollercoaster that would take me on a miserable, self-destructive ride for forty years.

Working through the protocol, I connected. Then cried. Then, as I was comforting ten-year-old me, my partner intruded and put a pillow in my hand. She told me to hold on to it like it was my little girl self. I did as she asked, and I lost the connection. I faked like I didn't, but I did.

The important thing I learned here was that the mind-body connection is internal. It comes from the client. Outside props disrupt the process. Other therapy techniques work from the outside in. Talk therapy or cognitive behavioral therapy start with the outer, more rational part of the brain and work their way slowly to what's buried in the deeper midbrain. This can take months or years. Mind-body allows the client to use the feelings in their body to go straight to that midbrain, into the trauma, no props needed.

THE REBIRTH

On our fifth and final day, Tillie and I were back together. Our assignment was to age-regress to gestationally four weeks old, after conception but before attaching to our mother's umbilical cord. A core self-meditation such as this is supposed to help clients experience "being," without thinking about "doing." The idea is for them to realize that just being makes them good enough.

Talk about new-agey! But at this point, my experience with brainspotting had been so positive, I was willing to go there.

Tillie said I was "out" for thirty minutes. To me, it felt like ten. I don't know if I was connected to my pre-birth self or not. What I do know is that I experienced a free-floating sensation that connected me to my creator. I realized on a deep level something I had never felt before: that He'd created me in His image, so I reflected His glory, His holiness, pure love, and goodness.

My concern over my sinful nature simply fell away. My original sin had been replaced with the more profound truth that I was inherently good. That I was worthy by the mere fact that I existed. That I didn't need to follow any rules or look a certain way or join a certain group or even be married.

It was powerful and empowering to feel comfortable with who I was, for the first time in my life.

RETURNING RENEWED

Each session had allowed me to revisit myself at critical junctures in my life and to re-parent myself through them. The things that happened to me weren't erased, but the fear and terror connected to my old memory of them were.

By the end of the training, I'd experienced what true connection feels like. Connection is what we as human beings use to get ourselves through life-threatening situations. We connect to each other for safety, protection, and comfort. Connection is what we're looking for when we're scared. If my mom had been able to provide connection for me, I would not have developed PTSD.

Through the re-parenting process, I found that inner connection I would use going forward to create a secure attachment to myself, a safe haven within me that no one and no trauma can ever take away. To this day, it's the place I go when I feel scared. I simply move my attention into myself and hold myself together until I calm my fears. And while I have many deep and rewarding friendships today, the attachment I value most is the one to myself. I am my own best friend.

Interestingly enough, I cemented my first two real and deep friendships in Tucson—Tillie and Avis. The walls of protection that had prevented me from forming intimate relationships my whole life had come down and I could be myself with them. Paradoxically, at the same time, I no longer felt that "neediness" to be liked by someone else. I believe that's because I had become a friend to myself.

I did not understand all this during the training or afterward. All I had was the experience itself. And simply from the feeling that experience produced, I knew down to my core that I could now find my way through anything as long as I trusted in who I was. I'd found my power.

Jim noticed the change in me right away. Years later, he told me, "Before Tucson, it was like you were either in neutral or had your foot on the brakes. You were resistant to everything I suggested. I always felt like I was pushing you along in life. After Tucson, you put your life in gear and began driving on your own. I loved watching you take charge of your life."

That's the way I felt, too. My anxiety had been replaced by confidence. I knew I could be a therapist—and a good one. With mind-body therapies, I'd be giving my clients the tools to find their healing within themselves—to access their own internal resources.

I was still having trouble reconciling my Christian beliefs with the idea that I could be my own source of unconditional love and acceptance. I'd struggle for the next several years with the conflict between my faith and the truths I'd found in Tucson. (Spoiler alert: Truth wins.)

EXERCISE

Connect to Nature Using Your Five senses

It's difficult to all of a sudden connect to another human being if you've not experienced what connection feels like. Many people experience a feeling of connection when they're in nature. So we can use nature as a stepping-stone to experience what connection feels like in our body.

- *Step one:* Use your imagination to choose a place in nature where you've been before and enjoyed.
- *Step two:* Start with five slow deep breaths, as you imagine yourself in this serene, beautiful place.
- *Step three:* Spend a full minute or two and notice what you see. Look up, look down, slowly turn around. Take note of the colors, shapes, and details of all the plants, sky, ground, ocean, or whatever you see. Take your time, breathe, and notice what you see.

- *Step four:* Take another minute or two and notice what you feel on your skin. Can you feel the sun on your face? The wind or breeze on your face? Take your shoes off and feel the earth. Reach your hands out and touch the plants, water, or rocks. Take your time, breathe, and notice what you feel.
- *Step five:* Take a minute or two and notice what you hear. Can you hear your footsteps? Can you hear birds or animals? Can you hear the water? Can you hear the plants moving? Take your time, breathe, and notice what you hear in this serene place.
- *Step six:* Take a minute or two and notice what you smell and taste. Smell the fresh air. Pick up the dirt or sand and smell it. Reach out and smell the trees and plants or seashells. Take your time, breathe, and notice what you smell and taste.
- *Step seven:* Last, but not least, notice what you feel, smell, see, and hear as you walk along in this beautiful place. This is what connection feels like. You belong here on earth, a part of all life.

Chapter 10

THE SPIRAL

Recovery from trauma is not a straight line to a specific destination. It's more like a journey along a spiral, each turn offering a new level of healing and insight to reach for and realize. When we make our way around that first curve of the spiral and get our initial glimpse of a life undistorted by trauma, it can seem as if maybe, finally we have things figured out. But just when we get comfortable, life more than likely shoves us back on the spiral and forces us to climb a little higher—albeit this time with more insight and self-awareness.

Tucson had definitely guided me around that initial curve. I was feeling good in my own skin for the first time in my life. I found work energizing, and I looked forward to seeing clients. Jim and I were doing better than ever. Both children were grown. Emma was married, with a one-year old. My life seemed to be on a glide path.

Then Mom would call. Her voice alone was enough to trigger me back into reactive trauma brain—back to when I was a child, when she was my world. Because I hadn't yet fully processed or re-parented my anxious attachment pattern, I still took on her moods as if they were my own. If she felt anxious or unhappy in any way, I would do anything to relieve her pain—and in doing so, relieve my own.

Since my father had died, my mother had been struggling emotionally. Making her happy had become increasingly difficult. Despite the fact that I spoke to her every day—and Jim and I visited her every weekend—she'd leave phone messages like this: "I guess no one is there to talk to me. I just wanted to know if you were still alive. I haven't heard from you. I could be dead, and no one would even care. It seems you are too busy for me. Please call and come visit."

If I'd been able to think rationally, I'd have concluded that her complaint was exaggerated and she was being manipulative. But as soon as I heard her voice, my stomach would twist in a knot. Clear thinking left my brain. I'd worry that she was lonely. I'd want to drive through two hours of stop-and-go, Southern California traffic to spend time with her to ease her loneliness and my anxiety.

Sometimes in movies, a mother says to her grown daughter, "You'll always be my little girl." It's meant lovingly, not literally. But for traumatized parents and children, such a statement isn't sentimental. It's how the parent continues to perceive the adult child. And how the adult child continues to behave.

After about five years of living alone, Mom started a campaign to move in with Jim and me. As she had done throughout my childhood, such campaigns consisted of undermining my confidence until I did as she wanted. She knew moving in with us would require us to buy a bigger home, so she started by taking digs at my current house and me.

"I wish you hadn't bought that house without asking me," she'd say. "It's too small. If you had a bigger house, I could have moved in and helped you out." Subtle, right?

Jim and I had bought the house several years earlier, when we had two teenagers at home. If it had not been too small then, it certainly wasn't too small now. Not to mention, I didn't need help and we liked our house.

But at the sound of her disapproval, none of those thoughts came to my mind. Despite my breakthroughs in Tucson, my brain headed straight to where it had been conditioned to go over a lifetime of Mom: self-doubt.

"Is it too small?" I wondered.

With little asides sprinkled here and there throughout our conversations over the next several months, she was able to nudge me exactly where she wanted me to go. My mind would reel: "Did we need to buy a new house?" "How could we make it happen?" "How much money would we need?" "Who should I talk to—a realtor? A mortgage lender?"

My brain then (as all our brains are skilled at doing) created rational arguments for doing the irrational thing I was about to do: "Jim and I wouldn't have to drive every weekend to visit her." "Mom would not be lonely any longer if we all lived together." And my biggest delusion of all: "My mom will be happy."

Before I knew it, Mom and I were house hunting. We found a four-bedroom with a downstairs bedroom and bath, where she could live. The house had two large living rooms and two dining areas—so lots of space to be alone and be together. She decided this was the house she wanted. Jim and I deferred to her judgment.

As we prepared to move, I felt the relief I'd craved. I imagined us living like "The Waltons," close together and oh so happy.

BREAKDOWN

Before the furniture was in place, Mom started complaining about the house. And automatically, I flew into reaction mode:

She complained about the floors, I bought rugs.

She complained about her bathroom, I bought new fixtures.

She complained about the backyard, I hired four landscapers to fix it to her liking. She fired them.

She complained about a wall in her bedroom, I called in a contractor, who looked at me like I was crazy when I told him what I wanted him to do. Then he very patiently—and without actually telling me I was crazy—explained that moving that wall made no sense and it would be prohibitively expensive.

Jim and I developed a ritual before bed. We'd lie there and talk about my mom. What we could do. If we could do it. What we could say.

We vented, discussed, and planned every night. I wanted my mom to be happy with us. I couldn't understand her anger.

No matter what I did, her disgust with the house continued to grow. One day she screamed, "I'm living like a caged dog!"

At that moment, some awareness on my part kicked in—after all, I had made some progress on the spiral. She was hardly living like a caged dog. This was a beautiful, spacious home. Her anger at the house made no sense. Why would anybody get mad at a house? It can't do anything to you. It can't hurt your feelings. It's just a house—one that *she* helped choose! For a few days, I was able to ignore her anger and demands. I stopped reacting to her.

But Mom would not be ignored. She upped the ante. Just as she'd traded in her complaints about loneliness for issues with the house, she now traded her house issues for physical ailments. And being the good daughter I was desperate to be, I could not ignore her physical pain.

Recreating our old pattern, she'd sit down with me in the kitchen and start talking. But this time her stories were about her aches and pains—and she had a slew of them. She told me, sometimes while crying, how she couldn't sleep. Sometimes she'd be suffering with some mysterious skin condition. Sometimes it was an undiagnosable pain—like a backache or headache.

As I listened to her, my mind reacted like a tornado. In short order, my life became all about solving Mom's disease du jour. I'd be on the phone with her doctor or on the internet looking for solutions for insomnia, eczema, acid reflux, swollen feet, food allergies, diarrhea, constipation, loss of hearing, just to name a few. Every day it seemed I was taking her to one appointment after another. We visited ophthalmologists, a cardiologist, a pulmonary specialist, a gastrointestinal specialist, and an orthopedist. With every doctor came a new prescription. I'd get them filled. She wouldn't take them. She'd complain of side effects. Nothing helped; nothing was ever good enough. And there was always something new.

Her voice and her pain took over my brain. My mom was miserable, and my triggered brain told me it was my responsibility to change that. I could have no relief until I did.

As I focused solely on her physical problems, I was falling apart. Though my stomach was in a constant knot, I gained thirty pounds in a few months and didn't even notice. My body became a reflection of her anxiety. There was no end to her misery, and I was the container she was dumping it all into.

As time went on, her problems only multiplied—and she used each as an opportunity to manipulate me. After three car accidents, she gave up driving, which meant I had to drive her everywhere. Rather than being thankful for the service, she used every trip to criticize my driving. From her perch in the passenger seat, she'd bark orders at me to speed up or stop here or take this road or that. In no time, I went from being a cautious, safe driver to a nervous wreck behind the wheel. I started cutting people off, running red lights, and driving erratically, things I'd never done in my life.

She didn't limit the criticism to my driving. When I'd start cooking, she'd come into the kitchen, hover, and direct me. I started second-guessing myself on recipes I'd made a thousand times. I'd think, "Uh-oh, she's not going to like what I'm doing." I'd worry that I boiled water too long or the frying pan I was using was too small. Again, she had me so afraid that I would do something "wrong"; she didn't like that I couldn't think straight. My mind was a mess.

To top it off, she wouldn't eat what I cooked. She'd find something wrong with it. In my subjugated state, I'd agree with her and say, "Let's order pizza." Hence, the thirty pounds.

Her criticism wasn't limited to me. My nearly two-year-old granddaughter, Elena, was living with us. Emma had recently left her husband and moved back home—and I loved having both of them there. One day, Mom and I were getting ready to take Elena shopping and then to lunch. We'd promised her a trip to the toy store.

Elena was all dressed, but I needed to run a brush through her hair.

As I struggled with some tangles, she played with her dolls and wiggled a little because I was pulling on her hair. My mom felt Elena was being too fussy.

"Elena, sit still so grandma can brush your hair," she said. "You'll look very pretty. Don't you want to look pretty?"

Elena kept pushing me away because, frankly, though I didn't mean to, I was kind of hurting her. My mom's frustration grew. I could feel her tension rising. I became quiet. Mom tried to take over the hair brushing, but Elena squirmed away. Mom yelled at her to come back and stand still. Elena stayed on her side of the room with her dolls.

So my mom angrily shouted at this toddler, "Fine, then you're not getting a toy from the store!"

Elena fell to the ground and cried in frustration.

My mom then stood over Elena and began mocking her, "Whaaa! Whaaa! How do you like it?! Whaaaaa!"

I froze. My mom's voice, as she mimicked and taunted my granddaughter, triggered me into FFFF. I couldn't move my feet. My thoughts raced, "Pick her up! Dorothy, go and pick Elena up and comfort her." But I could not. I was locked inside my body. Five seconds, ten seconds, fifteen seconds passed. I stood still. Finally, my feet moved. I picked Elena up.

As I walked away, Elena stared back at my mom angrily. She knew, even at two, that she'd been mocked, and she didn't like it.

Today, I understand that when my mom raged and mocked Elena, her brain had been hijacked back to a time when if she didn't obey, she might be killed by enemy soldiers. To mom, obedience was a survival skill—one she wanted her children, grandchildren, and now great grandchild to have. Controlling the people she loved, knowing they would obey when she gave them an order, was how she felt safe.

That evening when Jim and I held our Mom debrief, I told him what happened. Jim said, "Now you know how you were parented by your mom."

Before Tucson and my one turn on the spiral, I would not have had the self-awareness to understand the wisdom in Jim's statement. Now, I could and did. I hadn't thought of the incident that way. But Jim was right. A light bulb turned on in my head. I realized my mom mocked my driving and cooking just like she'd mocked Elena. She was triggering me into being helpless little Dorothy—who didn't know how to cook or drive or think straight. But unlike Elena, I didn't get angry with her. Instead, I became scared and looked to her for even more direction.

The next day, I couldn't get out of bed. I felt paralyzed. Hopeless. I became aware of my physical and mental deterioration, and that I lived in a constant state of panic and self-doubt. I knew this wasn't normal. I knew I was having a nervous breakdown.

I also knew that I needed to re-parent this part of me that had to do with my mother. But I'd need help to do it. I had been working as an intern therapist at a residential addiction recovery center for women, and I saw how helpful it was for people in recovery to be away from their home environment. I started to think, "Maybe I could go into rehab?"

TAKING ME (AND MOM) TO THE NEXT LEVEL

I found a health and wellness center for women in Vermont. I talked to Jim about me going away for four weeks. He practically pushed me out the door. I don't even remember what we told my mom.

During my time in Vermont, I rested and got lots of individual and group therapy. Separated from my mom, I became clear-headed. I was able to see that the issue was not my mom, but me. I needed to change or nothing in my life was going to be different. I had to pull myself out of our relational pattern. I had to learn to recognize when I was triggered. I had to draw and set boundaries with my mother. I had to gain more self-awareness, but more importantly, self-compassion.

So that's where I put my focus and effort for those four weeks away.

Once back in California, I knew I'd need more support to implement what I had learned, to prevent a relapse. I called a colleague, Kim, who practiced mind-body therapy and signed up to work with her. Our weekly sessions continued the work I'd begun in Vermont, re-parenting myself from the triggers and interactions I had with my mom. With Kim's support, I moved up the spiral once again, taking my healing to a deeper level.

At home, I worked my way through a list of strategies to create healthy boundaries for myself and my mom. Some worked. Some didn't. For instance, cooking my meals separately didn't work—it was wasteful and too much effort. But getting a part-time caregiver for Mom was a lifesaver. Thankfully, a friend of hers volunteered, so Mom couldn't reject her. And I got to enjoy three days a week to myself. Mom still challenged everything I did. But with four weeks of recovery and my work with Kim to give me strength, I didn't give up on my plan.

From my mom's perspective, though, my drawing boundaries and not engaging in our usual back-and-forth felt to her like I was pulling away. That scared her. Which triggered her into her fight mode. Growing up, I'd witnessed her wild temper aimed at my dad and my little brother, but never at me. Now, she was raging at me. To her shock and surprise, I did not freeze or dissociate, as was my pattern. I raged right back.

The first time Jim heard me raise my voice to my mother, he was shocked. I never yelled at anyone. He came running from upstairs. He stood between me and Mom like a referee, hands outstretched, knees bent, looking back and forth, ready to jump between us. "Hey, you okay? What's going on?" "Whoa, calm down."

I didn't stop. I felt powerful. I had a voice. I stayed present, held my boundary. It only took two or three more arguments at this decibel level for my mom to stop throwing her anger at me. Subconsciously, she'd learned—because I had taught her—that her go-to FFFF defensive strategy would no longer work with me.

My heart still ached when my mom was angry with me or in pain. I still felt like crying. But instead of giving into her and losing myself—which was not healthy for either of us—I practiced a little exercise one of the therapists in Vermont had taught me. I'd put my hand over my heart and say to myself, "My suffering is just as valid as your suffering."

Slowly but surely, I untangled myself from my mom's feelings and dysfunctional behaviors.

My boundary also helped my mom untangle herself from me and respect me as the responsible adult I was—the one she'd raised. I'm still amazed at her ability to change at age eighty-six. Though she likely was not consciously working toward personal development, I commend my mom for doing whatever it took to stay in relationship with me. Stamina and stubborn resilience were strengths she had to the end of her life.

One afternoon, months after we'd stopped having shouting matches, we were pulling out of the driveway. She was telling me how to drive, and I was ignoring her. Out of nowhere, she turned to me said, "I tell you these things because I love you."

That was her truth. She loved me. I knew it then and I know it today.

EXERCISE

What is a Boundary?

A boundary is an invisible wall that surrounds you. Imagine you're a house, and around your house is a fence. Your fence has only one exit and entrance. You have control over who you let in and who you keep out—and when.

How does this work in relationships? For most of my life, my mom and I shared an open gate policy. In psychology, this is called an enmeshed relationship. This meant my mom did not ask my permission to come through my gate, and I never asked her to leave. When she asked me to do something with or for her, I never said no.

When I came home from rehab in Vermont, I drew a new boundary with my mom. I took charge of my gate and my front yard. Sometimes I asked her to leave my front yard. Sometimes I didn't even let her through the gate. That scared her because unlimited access to me had always made her feel safe. When I closed the gate, she became angry. Eventually she stopped pestering me to get in. Over time, she learned to ask my permission to enter or waited for me to invite her in, which I did often once I had gained control of my gate.

Taking charge of your gate—defining your boundaries—starts with awareness of your current situation:

- If you have difficulty saying "no" to people, then you might find you have too many people in your front yard. So you may want to strengthen your boundary.
- If you have difficulty saying "yes" to people, then you might find people you'd like to know are missing from your front yard. So you might want to make your boundary a little more flexible.

Neither situation is right or wrong. The questions here are: Are you in control of who you let in, and when? Are the people in your front yard enhancing your life, distracting you from what you want, or draining you? One way to become more aware of your boundaries is to journal each day for a week on how many times you say "yes" and "no" when you interact with the people in your life.

This information is power. Once you can see where your boundaries are, you can redefine them to better meet your needs.

Chapter 11

AN IDENTITY OF MY OWN

As taxing as my mind-body therapy sessions with Kim could be, I always felt better for them. I could see the progress in myself and in my life. There was no judgment in therapy, only curiosity. I didn't have to hide or be ashamed. Rather than hand my childhood trauma over to Jesus (which I came to see as basically ignoring it), I embraced my trauma—all of it. I took a good, honest look at it and re-parented myself through it. Week after week, session after session, the hold my past once held was loosening and clearing the way for me to become me.

Becoming less judge-y and more accepting of myself made me less judge-y and more accepting of others. I could no longer believe that people who weren't Christian were going to hell. I no longer saw homosexuality or any kind of sexuality or gender identity as a sin either. I also tossed out the notion that God ranked women below men and children below women. Aren't we all made in the image of God?

Though I was questioning beliefs I'd held for decades, I still considered myself a Christian. I continued to read my Bible every day and have my quiet time with God. These sessions, however, were becoming increasingly uncomfortable due to my growing self-awareness. I noticed that I would latch on to certain Bible verses and hold myself up to them and to the perfectionistic expectations they engendered.

I'd compare myself to Jesus or to his disciples. Then, I'd worry that I wasn't living up to what God wanted. Self-doubt would creep in. Then shame. Before I knew it, my reliable old trauma phrase "What's wrong with me?" was running through my brain on a continuous loop.

One day, when I caught myself mid-trigger, I took the opportunity to get curious. I asked myself why I began each day doing something that upset me. I also wondered why twenty-five years of following Jesus hadn't brought me the healing I'd found in only a few years of psychotherapy.

The whole purpose of quiet time with God was to start each day in the right frame of mind. To my church's way of thinking, that meant to conform myself to be more like Christ—also known as the sanctification process. Through reading scripture, I was opening myself to the power of the Holy Spirit and the word of God, so they could transform my sinful nature into something holy, pure, and pleasing to God.

And there it was. No wonder I felt split down the middle. Believing I needed to "transform my sinful nature" into something "pleasing to God" was completely in conflict with what I was doing in therapy. In therapy, I was welcoming and accepting all of me, including the sinful parts. I wasn't trying to become anything or anyone but me.

I realized my daily Bible reading didn't support my recovery from trauma. So I decided to take a break from it. I told myself that when I was done healing, I'd return to quiet time with God. That's how I did it when my first therapist Anne asked me to journal. So I placed my Bible on my nightstand with every intention of returning to it eventually.

FROM LIMBO TO LIBERATION

In therapy with Kim, I learned to access and feel my feelings fully. I learned what they had to tell me, and then to let go of them if they needed to go. Week by week, layer by layer, I peeled away the false assumptions I'd been living under for decades—including that there was something wrong with me. By accepting and exploring my feelings—instead of judging them—my thoughts became congruent and integrated. I no longer needed to compartmentalize and split as I had done before (remember Godly Dorothy and Deviant Dorothy). Thus, my emotional resilience grew stronger. A slight by someone, or a mistake by me, no longer sent me down a path of self-loathing and despair.

As I climbed higher on the spiral, I found my agency and autonomy. I was now in a trusting and loving relationship with myself. I discovered my own identity apart from my mom's forceful identity. In psychological terms, this is called differentiation of the self.

I also began to see myself apart from my Christian identity. After all, my Christian identity had formed around my traumatized personality—which I was now discarding layer by layer. As my trauma lifted, so did my need for the routine, certainty, and security that Christianity had given me. The meek, obedient, and dependent woman that trauma and Christianity had shaped was being replaced by the real me—who could still be timid, but now was independent in thought and voice.

Somewhere during this time, it occurred to me that I'd always thought Christianity was about unconditional love. But now I could see that Jesus's love—at least the way my church presented it—was very conditional and always had been. I came to see that the answers I sought for my life were not going to be found in my Bible. My Christian belief system had been a lifeline for me at one time. But now, it was a barrier to my continued growth.

One day, as I sat on my bed, I looked over at my Bible. It had been sitting on my nightstand unopened for a year. I asked myself, "Do I believe any of this anymore?" My answer was "no." I picked up my Bible, looked at it, and threw it in the trash.

I was no longer a Christian.

I don't know that I would be so extreme today. But at the time, throwing away my Bible was something I needed to do to move on. I was angry, which is a normal phase of grief. And losing faith in my religion constituted a profound loss for me, worthy of grieving.

I felt I'd been tricked by my religion. I mourned the decades I devoted to it. All the years I hadn't allowed myself to be curious about the world. All the wasted effort put into making my children Christians, instead of building authentic connection with them. My Bible had been so foundational to my relationship with God: He talked to me through His word, and I talked back to him in prayer, every day. So I needed that dramatic act of throwing away my Bible, at that moment, in order to truly break away.

GETTING TO KNOW ME

At first, I didn't tell anyone except Jim. It turns out he was way ahead of me.

He'd been struggling with our faith since his days at Covenant College. The more involved he became in the church and the more he read, studied, and observed, the more he couldn't help but note the inconsistencies in the theology and witness the hypocrisy in the way our church practiced it.

For instance, to Jim, the Bible was so obviously not the literal word of God—yet that's what we were asked to believe. Creationism made no sense—yet that's what we were asked to defend. He absolutely could not understand why a woman could not lead a congregation. And then, of course, he had been there when we had so many issues with Emma, when our church community not only had no answers but abandoned us. All of this slowly pushed Jim to question his faith.

Still, he knew how much the church meant to me. So although he was a doubter, he participated. It just didn't hold the meaning for him it once had.

Now that I wasn't Christian, the first thing on my agenda was to figure out what I was. What did I believe? My research consisted of listening to a lot of podcasts on being an agnostic, atheist, or "spiritual but not religious." I'd heard some free-thinkers call themselves agnostic-atheists too. What I learned is it comes down to whether or not one believes in the supernatural.

So I made a list of everything I could think of that was supernatural— God, Jesus, the Holy Spirit, angels, demons, aliens, fairies, zombies, magic, witches, Santa Claus, ghosts, dragons, heaven, hell, eternal life, etc. Then, I went through the list. If I believed in anything on it, I'd be an agnostic. If I didn't, I'd be an atheist.

Turns out I was an atheist. I ran straight to Jim.

"Jim! Jim! I'm an atheist!"

'Noooooo," he said.

'Yeeeeessssss," I said.

"Well, don't tell anybody."

He was right. Our life was still bound up in our church. Leaving was going to require careful thought. Leaving my religion was about more than not going to church for me. All my adult life I'd depended on Christianity to form my ideas, my political beliefs, my relationships, my business practice, my everything. I listened to Christian music. Watched Christian TV. I got my news from a Christian channel. We took Christian vacations. Now I'd have to find all these things for myself. Make my own choices. Choose my own tastes. I would have to form a new identity—for real. I needed to find and define my self.

We also had to be careful how we explained this new reality to the people in our life. All our family (except our children) and friends were evangelical Christians. They would be sincerely afraid for our eternal souls. We had to consider their feelings as well as our own.

As we processed this new state of being and what to do next, Jim and I talked for hours and hours. We shared our fears, our hopes, our "what-nows?" Of course, our shared fervor for Christianity had drawn us to each other in the beginning. And now, all these years on, our deconversion from Christianity would see us become even closer—because now we were both on a path to becoming our authentic selves.

I would have left the church with or without Jim because it was so important to my individuation. But having a partner for the journey—especially one as smart and open and accepting of me as Jim—made it so much easier and even more meaningful.

EXERCISE

What Do You Believe?

Examining which supernatural things I did or didn't believe in helped me get clear on whether I was going to be agnostic or atheist.

Here are the things I questioned (some of which I mentioned earlier):

1. God
2. Satan
3. Heaven
4. Hell
5. Higher Power
6. Angels
7. Ghosts
8. Demons
9. Miracles
10. Reincarnation
11. Santa Claus
12. Unicorns
13. Fairies
14. Trolls
15. Monsters
16. Spirits
17. Soul
18. The love of the universe
19. Magic
20. Witches
21. Warlocks
22. The Occult
23. Evil

24. Curses and Spells
25. Eternal Life

Often, we believe in things just because we always have. We don't really know why. And we don't take the time to question them. So I invite you to make a list of your beliefs—whatever they are—and ask yourself if you really do believe them or are they just something you accepted your whole life. This is a great exercise to get to know yourself better. Most clients find this exercise helps them to get clear and strengthen some beliefs, while letting let go of others.

To take a closer look at your beliefs, follow these steps:

- *Step one:* Make a list of the things you believe in.
- *Step two:* Think about each one. Ask yourself if this is still your belief or not, and why. Your answers might surprise you. Remember, there is no right or wrong here. No judgment.
- *Step three:* For each item you list, write in your journal: I believe in _____ because _____. Or I do not believe in _____ because _____.
- *Step four:* Now that you've examined your beliefs, what insights have you gleaned about yourself? In what ways do you better understand yourself?

Chapter 12

INTERGENERATIONAL HEALING

If I were to break the chains of trauma and become this "me" I was working so hard in therapy to discover, there was one more false identity I needed to expose. That identity was me as I appeared in my children's eyes. My therapist suggested I open up to my children about who I'd been when they were little. Where I felt I'd made errors raising them. To tell them I'm sorry, and that I'm working to do better moving forward.

I was petrified at the thought!

"What? You want me to actually apologize to my children?" I said.

"Yes, that's exactly what I want you to do."

"What if they reject me? What if they are angry with me?" I said.

My therapist explained that if I truly wanted to have a meaningful relationship with them, this is where I needed to begin. She gave me suggestions on how to broach the subject. She encouraged me to be honest, and to ask for their forgiveness. She assured me that this would be very healing for them.

Emma was twenty-seven at the time, Dustin twenty-four. I wanted to do it. But I didn't think I could do it face to face. So I wrote them an email. Then with my heart in my throat, I hit send. This is what I wrote:

Dear Emma and Dustin,

These are my greatest hopes and desires for you today as I write this letter:

For you to love and accept yourselves

For you to feel comfortable with who you are

And for you to trust your intuition to be your inner guide through life.

These desires are quite different from when I was a Christian. When I was your Christian mom, my greatest desires for you were:

For you to recognize your need for God

For you to believe in Jesus to save you from hell

And for you to find your purpose and guidance through faith in Christ.

I don't think that any of these desires has anything to do with my love for you. I love you now and I loved you then. What HAS changed is my love for myself.

Over the last six years, I've been healing in therapy from my childhood trauma of emotional and sexual abuse. At the same time, I've been de-converting from Christianity to atheism.

I know you've felt the change. Both of you have mentioned it to me.

Remember in the movie, The Matrix, when Neo was given a choice to either take the red pill and awaken to the reality of how his brain was being hijacked? Or he could take the blue pill to remain in the fake dream world of the matrix?

Six years ago, my therapist held out a red pill to me. If I chose to take it, I would awaken to the reality of my childhood experiences and face my fears. If I chose the blue pill, I would retreat back to where I had been living for the past twenty-five years...into the Jesus Wonderland Matrix.

I chose the red pill. Guess what I found? The truth has set me free. (Okay, I'll concede the Bible has some gems of wisdom.)

So you might be asking why this is important for you? I hope that when you read some of my story, you will come to understand yourselves better.

I know that you both struggle with hearing critical and insecure voices in your head. Let me tell you where those voices come from. Those critical voices come from me (and your traumatized dad). We put those in your head when you were little because at that time we believed that at your core, you were sinful, bad, and rebellious. We were so wrong. You were normal, good kids.

Where did this wrong belief come from? You might ask. Well, partly these critical voices were put into our heads from our parents. And partly from our Christian belief in original sin. Here's a little formula to remember...

Childhood Trauma + Christian Faith = Parents who pass on their trauma into their children, from generation to generation to generation. (From Grandma and Grandpa to Mom and Dad to Emma and Dustin.)

You see, that shame that I felt from my childhood, I misunderstood as sin. For most of my life I felt bad, perverted, sinful, scared, anxious, empty, and unworthy of love because of the shame that I carried within me from sexual abuse when I was a child.

Christianity taught me how to manage those bad feelings through spiritual practices like praying and reading my Bible. The Bible taught me to deny myself (and my past), pick up my cross, and follow Jesus. I also prayed a lot as a way to escape the pain of inadequacy that I felt. Remember how I used to sleep a lot and take a lot of naps? Yup, I know we reframed it as a family quirk, but this was another way I escaped.

These icky feelings increased over time, so that by the time you were children, I was expending a lot of energy managing these yucky feelings. I had PTSD but misdiagnosed it and misinterpreted it as my wicked, sinful, warped, evil nature.

The only coping tools I had were my spiritual practices of prayer, Bible study, and church, which at least helped me feel good about myself some of the time. As you can see, this didn't leave much energy for being your mom. So you naturally felt insecure, confused, and alone.

The only solution that I knew of was for you to take the blue pill. Your dad and I were both living in the Jesus Wonderland of the Matrix. We were desperate for you both to be there with us.

You forced us to step out of the matrix once in a while just by being normal kids, which we really didn't like. So we yelled at you and argued with you and became very angry with you. We felt hurt that you didn't want to join us. This was not your fault, even though we made you feel like it was your fault.

But because we had the advantage of being your parents, we used every parental trick we could think of to get you to accept the Jesus Wonderland Matrix. We used our whole arsenal of spiritual weapons: We prayed. We recruited our family's prayers. We dragged you to church. We forced you to go to Christian youth camp. We sent you to Christian counselors. We sent you to Christian behavioral modification programs. We shamed you. We sent you into therapy (not us, just you)...

Emma and Dustin, I am so so sorry. It was I who was broken and needed help, not you. I know your dad feels the same. Does this help you to understand yourselves better? I hope so.

I can see you clearly now the pain of the past is gone.

I can love you for who you are because I can love myself.

I can accept you because I can accept myself.

I'd like to leave you with some things I know for sure...(yeah, I know this is an Oprah interview question)...

- *~ Love covers over a multitude of fear.*
- *~ You and I are good enough just the way we are.*
- *~ All life here on earth is the miracle, so Live YOUR Life and BE the miracle.*

~ *Human beings are born good.*
~ *Choosing the red pill was not easy, but it definitely was worth it!*

I love you,

~mom

The replies I got back from both of them were sweet. But they were both confused. They put the blame on themselves for any trouble or problems they'd had growing up and even now. Being a therapist and a trauma survivor, I shouldn't have been surprised that both my children were having trouble with the notion that Jim and I hadn't been perfect parents. We needed to sit down and talk.

FALSE IDOLS

It's typical for children to show resistance to blaming their parents. This is especially true for children brought up in households where the parents are presented as infallible and to be obeyed. Which precisely describes how Christian mom (me) raised Emma and Dustin. So it's no wonder they idolized me (whether they knew it or not), just as I had idolized my mom, just as Jim had idolized his parents.

As we talked, I got them both to see that I was a person and one who makes lots of mistakes. I explained to them how my imperfect parenting played a role in some of the hurdles they had to overcome in childhood and some of the negative thinking about themselves they continue to deal with to this day. It would take many more conversations, but eventually I was able to bust their "mother-idol myth," making room for a new, more real relationship among all of us.

Then, to my surprise, Emma responded to my letter with her own:

Dear Mom,
Thank you for your letter.

I remember when you first started your therapy, you told me it was your fault that I had the struggles I did, and I said "Cool, it's not my fault!" as a joke. But I realize now those words you spoke hold so much truth.

In your letter, you said your desires for me have changed but your love has not. You loved me when you were a Christian, and you love me now that you're not. I one-hundred percent believe this. In fact, because I knew you loved me growing up, as my Christian mother, it was hard to understand why I struggled. When you think about the kids that go "bad," they are usually ones with a broken home.

I had no visible issues in my home. My parents were still together, and they were hard-working, loving, Christian parents. We went to church on Sundays, spent holidays with extended family, and even had family game night on the weekends. So why did I feel inadequate? Why did I have negative self talk? Why was I so insecure? Why did I go "bad"? Until you started your own therapy and were able to pass on some new knowledge to me, my questions went unanswered.

When I had my daughter a little more than six years ago, I hadn't resolved those issues quite yet, but I at least had my motherly instinct kick in. This led to a series of events and ended with me moving back in with you and dad for about two years. For this I am grateful, because living with you is when I think you were able to pass on your healing to me.

I was twenty-two years old, recently separated (later to be divorced), working full-time, had a one-year-old, and I had just moved back in with my parents. Life wasn't exactly going the way I would have liked. You were going through therapy and sharing different parenting techniques with me. From what you've said, it's what you wish you had known when raising Dustin and me.

One of the most impactful things you taught me was that I needed to be there for Elena emotionally. That she should have a secure attachment to me. I didn't know this!! Why didn't I know this? It seemed so simple! I now realize it is because I didn't get *that with you or dad as a kid. And that is where my "issues" came from. Even though I had two loving parents, they were dealing with their own "issues;" they were emotionally unavailable and shoving Christianity down my throat because it is what helped them deal. But it wasn't helping me deal.*

I'm so freaking happy that you went through your own therapy, because it helped me come into my own self without me even realizing it!!

During those two years of living with you as an adult raising my own child, I was able to get that love, validation, or whatever it was that I didn't get as a kid. And to be honest, you didn't do anything super different than when I was a kid. We talked, hung out, and you were my mom. Just like when I was a kid. But you were YOU. I felt that you were you; and I felt that you were okay with who I was, whoever that was going to be.

I know that is why I am able to be myself now. I know it, not because you've told me, but because I experienced it. I felt it happen. I enjoyed every minute of it. And I can reflect back on it and realize that is what did it. It's hard to explain, and I'm sure you could explain it with all your therapy terms, but all I know is that those insecurities I felt as a child/young adult are no longer there, or at least not nearly as strong.

I am confident in myself. I am confident in the decisions I make. I am confident in the mistakes I make. I've realized I'm very social. I love being around people, but I also know I need alone time to recharge. I'm not afraid to try new things. I'm not afraid to fail.

I KNOW MYSELF AND WHO I AM.

I realize that who I am comes from inside me and can be influenced from who and what I surround myself with. I also realize that who I am can constantly change. Change is a huge part of life. Being able to deal and cope with change has been liberating.

I LOVE THAT I KNOW MYSELF; I LOVE THE CONFIDENCE

THAT COMES WITH IT AND THE ANXIETY THAT HAS GONE AWAY.

Knowing myself has helped me realize what I want out of life, for now anyways.

I know I want to be there for my daughter. I want to drop her off and pick her up from school. I want to take her to her activities. I want to help her with her homework. I want to enjoy a night out or happy hour with my friends. I want to live in Texas. I want to work part-time now while my daughter is young and pursue my career more once she's older. I want to meet a man I can enjoy life with (and I'm okay with waiting for that to happen). I want to believe in God.

Without those insecurity voices in my head, I've been able to create the life I want to live. I know I would not have been strong enough five years ago to make the same decisions I've been able to make today. Going from that scared, insecure twenty-two-year-old that just moved back with her parents to where I am now, living the exact life I want to, is a little surreal to think about.

I'm not shocked you are an atheist now. It was a long process, I sort of watched you undergo and I actually feel indifferent to it now. I don't have a ha! satisfaction feeling. I don't feel sad, mad, or embarrassed. I'm just so happy you are able to be you! And if your leaving the Christian faith has something to do with it, then I'm glad. Mostly for selfish reasons, because it has enabled me to be me!

I still call myself a Christian. I will admit, I do feel Christianity is a socially acceptable status to claim. Many will identify as Christian without doing much or any of the Christian practices. And to be honest, I like that. I want to believe in God, so I do. But I don't want to go to church every Sunday or follow all the rules, so I don't. Five years ago, I would probably have felt scared to admit that; afraid of people's judgments and even more afraid of my own inner judgments. But today I have no problem saying... I believe in God, but on Sunday I want to sleep in and not go to church. And if some-

one wants to have an opinion on that, cool! You do you because imma do me!

Lastly, I don't blame you for getting it wrong when I was a kid. Just like it's not my fault, it's yours; it's not your fault, it's your parents.' And it's not their fault, it's their parents.' I'm just so happy you broke the cycle, I'm glad you chose the red pill and not the blue pill. I'm happy I get to be present for myself. I'm happy I get to be present for my own daughter. I'm happy I get to watch her grow into her own self.

Love you, Mom,
Emma

PASSING THE HEALING ON

As you can imagine, I've read and reread this letter many times with tears. Today, as I type it into this manuscript, I'm again filled with joy and wonder at the wisdom and the beautiful secure voice that comes across in those words. Yes, we broke the cycle. We broke it by tending to the emotional neglect we experienced as children. We took responsibility for healing ourselves. First me. And then I passed what I'd learned to my children. Emma now has it to pass to Elena.

As an added bonus, both Emma and Dustin trust me not to judge but to explore with them. They come to me to talk over important things in their lives.

Like when Emma was set to marry a man we all liked and then seemingly out of the blue, called it off. "It's strange," Emma told me, "I purposefully chose him because he was opposite of my ex-husband. I tried so hard not to make another mistake. And here I am, after three years, having the same relationship I had with my ex-husband."

She realized that to change her relationship patterns, she had more work to do on herself. Years later, she let me know that she'd found the permission within herself to break up with her fiancée because she saw me giving myself permission to live the life I wanted. That's intergenerational healing.

And recently when we were on the phone, she was telling me about the man she's currently dating. "I like him just because I like him. And not because he likes me." That's secure attachment speaking.

We're never too old to do this work and pass the healing on. My children were adults when my healing journey began. Still, my new understanding of myself brought honesty, clarity, and curiosity into all our lives. It enabled Emma and Dustin to create new meaning around their own childhood experiences. Changing how they understand themselves and benefiting their lives to this day, as well as benefiting their children and all future generations to come.

EXERCISE

A Note for the Next Generation

Write a letter to your children. Think about what it was like for your child to be raised by you. The positive and the negative. Write from your heart. Apologize for your mistakes.

You don't have to send it or give it to them. You can write it in your journal, just for you. Simply taking this time to think through their experience of you will help your relationship as you move forward.

It's never too late to repair a parent-child relationship. Remember your child is attached to you and needs you. I have found in my practice—as in my life—that children are very forgiving.

Chapter 13

THRIVING

The last two years of my mom's life, I'm happy to say, were good ones for both of us. Separate identities no longer enmeshed emotionally, our relationship was unburdened by trauma and triggers, and so it was able to mature. As difficult as it was at times to have my mother living with us, I never would have healed to the depths I did if she had not moved in.

I'd also become a full adult partner in my marriage—a person and personality distinct from Jim. Once I became a licensed marriage and family therapist, I stopped working for his law firm and opened my own private practice. Jim continued working as an attorney for a few more years, while he earned his doctor of psychology degree (PsyD). Eventually, he did leave the law, though he didn't go far. He became a forensic psychologist for our county's family law court.

I can honestly say I was thriving.

THE WORK OF HEALING IS NEVER DONE—AND THAT'S A GOOD THING

While that would make a tidy place to end this book, there is no such thing as tidy or an end when it comes to healing trauma—mine or yours. And I wouldn't want to leave you with that impression.

My trauma-driven life had been all about surviving—stuffing my feelings, ignoring problems, checking-out emotionally from any triggering situation to make it through the day, the hour, and sometimes the moment. However, that doesn't mean my thriving life has been all joy all the time, with everything going my way.

Healing from trauma did not (and has not) relieved me of life's challenges or even my own triggers fully. The difference is that now I've learned to recognize what I feel, and I know what to do about it. I also know that within each challenging situation is usually an opportunity for deeper healing and more growth—another level on that spiral.

When I opened my practice, for instance, I was full of confidence in my ability to help my clients. What I hadn't given much thought to was actually getting those clients. A new challenge, you might say. For someone as shy and unfamiliar with people and business as I was, it was an out-and-out obstacle.

My first instinct was to avoid the discomfort (and triggers) of typical marketing activities and opt for a passive approach to promotion. I signed up with insurance companies, so I'd show up on their in-network lists, and I put my profile on popular search sites for therapists—both solid ways to reach potential clients. Also the same ways every therapist in California was using. I didn't stand out much. I got a few clients from these efforts, but not enough to keep my doors open.

If I wanted a successful practice, there was no avoiding a more active approach. I would need to put myself and my services out there in public—for people to judge. I would need to network—otherwise known as talking to people I didn't know, and worse, convincing them to give me money. Needless to say, I was triggered all over the place. My fear of being seen, my insecurities, and my feelings of not being good enough were on the rise.

But now, when I felt all these discomforts in my body, I knew what they were—nothing more than old narratives I told myself about old wounds. They weren't the truth, then or now. And I knew what to do. Get quiet. Get in touch with where this discomfort was in my body. And re-parent the inner child who was expressing the pain. Then, comfort and hold myself. Talk to myself about the situation at the moment, not my situation fifty years ago. Solve my issue if I could. Ask for help if it was needed.

Using this method over and over again, I processed whatever trauma surfaced, and I relieved my discomfort. With each repetition, the neural pathways in my brain on the journey toward healing got stronger and deeper, until they became my brain's default pattern, replacing my FFFF response. That's when I began to thrive.

Yes, I was still scared by stuff that had always scared me, but not so frightened that I froze and couldn't live out the life I wanted for myself. And if I wanted to have my own practice, I needed to gain confidence speaking to strangers, as well as marketing and operating a business.

So I joined Toastmasters. There, I not only found the opportunity to continue to process the discomfort that public speaking provoked, but I also became a pretty good speaker. Which helped me promote my practice and led to other business opportunities. Things I never imagined I could do, like give talks, be a guest on podcasts, and present at workshops and seminars.

I also got a business coach and joined a mastermind group to learn marketing and operations. As part of that mastermind, I found myself flying across the country four times a year to collaborate with other business owners from all over the world—some of whom I lean on for ideas, problem-solving, and friendship to this day. Yes, I learned how to run my practice and market my services. But more than that, I developed the mindset of an entrepreneur, which has meant everything in the success of my practice and in my ability to serve my clients well.

CREATING YOUR OWN PATH TO HEALING— THE PARENT TOOL

All of this growth was made possible by my being able to use the resources already within me and re-parent myself whenever and wherever I needed to. To make this easier for me and my clients (and now you), I developed a tool that uses the acronym "PARENT" and leads you step-by-step through the process. You can use it on the spot as you experience emotional pain. Or some clients use it every morning to see what comes up for them.

To try it, set aside at least ten minutes. Get some place quiet and simply move through the steps:

- *Step one:* P is for pause. Pause when you notice something is wrong or just feels off. Stop talking. Stop doing. Stop thinking. Stop analyzing. Stop fixing. Be still. Take a slow, deep breath. Then take another. And another.
- *Step two:* A is for Accept. Resolve to accept yourself—including your inner child. Hold your hands palms-up to welcome your younger self. Gesture for your little one to come in. Say to your little one: "It's okay. I'm not mad at you. You're not in trouble. It's not your fault. You can come to me. I'm here for you. Come to me."
- *Step three:* R is for Reside. Reside within your body. Rub your hands gently on your chest. Feel your lungs breathing. Feel your heart beating. Feel your head, neck, shoulders, arms, and hands. Feel your back muscles, legs, and feet. Be present to the sensations of your body.
- *Step four:* E is for Express. Express your pain. First, identify where you feel any pain, pressure, or tightness. You might also feel aches, pin pricks, numbness, bloating, nausea, or a general heaviness. Then sit with the discomfort until you connect to it. This is where your inner-child or little one is expressing their feelings and their needs. Breathe into it.
- *Step five:* N is for Nurture. Your inner child has expressed the pain; now you need to tend to it. Put your hands on your heart and say to your little one, "I'm here for you. I'm here to help you. How can I help?" And then wait for an answer.
- *Step six:* T is for Trust. Trust your body has healed you. Breathe into your heart and body, and ask: What insight have I gained?

What have I learned from this experience today? A word, a sentence, or a phrase will do. Say your insight aloud five times and then write it down. By asking your body what you've learned, you're integrating the new experience from your midbrain and base stem into your neocortex. In other words, by putting words to your experience, you're taking your healing from your unconscious or automatic brain into your conscious brain. You're creating a new, preferred neural pathway.

If you choose to do this every day, you're likely to find you're better able to meet your own emotional needs and that your insecure attachment pattern transforms to a more secure attachment. You should also start to feel better, less reactive, and more in charge of your life. You should find healing. (If you want to take your healing from intergenerational trauma further, feel free to contact me through my website at www.dorothyhusen.com or find a mind-body therapist in your area who can guide you through the re-parenting process and attachment issues.)

NOW, I HAVE A STORY. AND YOU DO TOO.

For most of my life, I thought I had no story of my own. My mother had a story. Jim had a story, too. But trauma made me think I was nothing more than a secondary character in their stories—and in my life. Always fading into the background. Always reacting to, never causing the action.

But here I am. With story enough to fill a book and a life of my own making. A life that's fulfilling to me and a healthier influence on my children, grandchild, and everyone I love. It didn't happen overnight. It certainly wasn't a straight upward trajectory toward recovery and realization. There have been good days and bad days—and my guess is that will continue to be so. But now the days of my life are mine. Days in which I have autonomy. Days in which I make the decisions good or bad—not my mom, not Jesus, not Jim, and not trauma.

You have your own story, too. It's inside of you right now, waiting for you to begin your healing journey. To peel away the falsehoods of intergenerational trauma. To bring your life into clear focus. To find compassion, love, and acceptance for yourself; all of yourself. To thrive.

Acknowledgements

Thank you, Emma and Dustin, for revealing my insecurities and then staying with me through my struggle to become your mom.

Thank you, Jim, for your never-ending kindness, support, and encouragement to find my own story.

Thank you, Beth, my friend and editor, for planting the seed for this book after I told you my story, and you said to me, "You need to write a book." And then you patiently guided me for the next three years and told me after each draft, "It's really good and you need to re-write it again."

Thank you, Mom and Dad, for surviving your traumas and for always being there for me.

And lastly, thank you, my little Dorothys:, my toddler, my six-year-old, my ten-year-old, and my fourteen-year-old. Your survival made it possible for me to thrive. I love you all.

Endnotes

Chapter 1
American Psychiatric Association, *Diagnostic and Statistical Manual of Mental Disorders – 5th Edition*. (American Psychiatric Association, 2013), page 271

Chapter 2
Kent Hoffman, Glen Cooper, Bert Powell, *Raising a Secure Child: How Circle of Security Parenting Can Help You Nurture Your Child's Attachment, Emotional Resilience, and Freedom to Explore*. (The Guilford Press, 2017)

Chapter 6
1 Cor. 6:18 (New International Version, Biblica, 1978)
Hebrews 13:4 (NIV)
Mathew 5:28 (NIV)
Leviticus 18:22 (*Amplified Bible Classic Edition, The Lockman Foundation*, 1987)
1 Cor. 6:9-11 (NIV)
Colossians 3:5 (NIV)
Romans 7:1–20 (NIV)

Chapter 7
Romans 6:23 (NIV)

Chapter 9
David Grand, *Brainspotting: The Revolutionary New Therapy for Rapid and Effective Change*. (Sounds True, 2013)

About the Author

Dorothy Husen is a mind-body psychotherapist and coach. She specializes in working with people suffering from chronic pain due to childhood trauma, abuse, or ongoing stress. She helps them access their own internal resources, so they can heal at the emotional root of their pain and live their true lives.

Dorothy teaches several online workshops and courses. For upcoming programming go to http://www.dorothyhusen.com/online-courses.

Dorothy also works one-on-one with clients. For a free consult, make an appointment on her calendar at www.dorothyhusen.com/contact.

www.ingramcontent.com/pod-product-compliance
Lightning Source LLC
Chambersburg PA
CBHW072019110526
44592CB00012B/1369